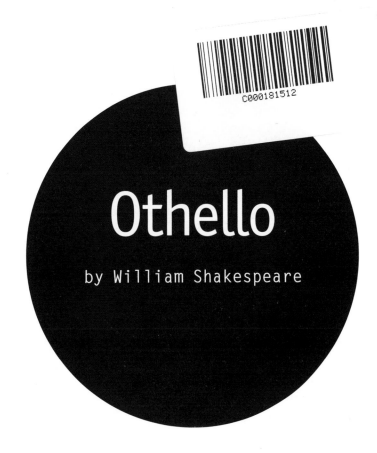

Othello

by William Shakespeare

Peter Bunten

Series Editors:
Nicola Onyett and Luke McBratney

HODDER
EDUCATION
AN HACHETTE UK COMPANY

The publisher would like to thank the following for permission to reproduce copyright material:

Acknowledgements:

William Shakespeare: from *Othello* (1623); **p.39: A.C. Bradley:** *Shakespearean Tragedy: Lectures on Hamlet, Othello, King Lear, Macbeth* (Macmillan, 1904); **p.40: Anne Ridler (ed.):** *Shakespearean Criticism 1935–1970* (Oxford University Press, 1970); **p.40: Karen Newman in J.E. Howard and M.F. O'Conner (eds):** '"And wash the Ethiop White": Femininity and the Monstrous in Othello', *Shakespeare Reproduced: The Text in History* (Routledge, 1987) Reprinted by permission from Taylor & Francis Group.

Photo credits:

p.4 © Johan Persson/ ArenaPAL/TopFoto; **p.12** © Nigel Norrington/ ArenaPAL/ TopFoto; **p.16** © Nigel Norrington/ ArenaPAL/TopFoto; **p.21** © World History Archive/ TopFoto; **p.27** © Elliott Franks/ ArenaPAL/TopFoto; **p.29** © Everett Collection/ REX/ Shutterstock; **p.30** © Nigel Norrington/ ArenaPAL/TopFoto; **p.32** © Everett Collection/REX/Shutterstock; **p.35** © Johan Persson/ ArenaPAL/TopFoto; **p.41** © Johan Persson/ ArenaPAL/TopFoto; **p.48** © Nigel Norrington/ ArenaPAL/ TopFoto; **p.51** © Fine Art Images/ HIP/ TopFoto

Although every effort has been made to ensure that website addresses are correct at time of going to press, Hodder Education cannot be held responsible for the content of any website mentioned. It is sometimes possible to find a relocated web page by typing in the address of the home page for a website in the URL window of your browser.

Orders: please contact Bookpoint Ltd, 130 Milton Park, Abingdon, Oxon OX14 4SB. Telephone: (44) 01235 827720. Fax: (44) 01235 400454. Lines are open 9.00–17.00, Monday to Saturday, with a 24-hour message answering service. Visit our website at www.hoddereducation.co.uk.

© Pete Bunten 2016

First published in 2016 by

Hodder Education

An Hachette UK Company,

Carmelite House, 50 Victoria Embankment

London EC4Y 0DZ

Impression number	5	4	3	2	1
Year	2020	2019	2018	2017	2016

Cover photo (and throughout) © Dima Sobko/123RF.com

Typeset in Univers LT Std 47 Light Condensed 11/13 pt by Integra Software Services Pvt. Ltd., Pondicherry, India

Printed in Italy

A catalogue record for this title is available from the British Library

ISBN 978 1 4718 5392 0

Contents

Why read this guide?

The purpose of this A-level Literature Guide is to enable you to organise your thoughts and responses to the text, to deepen your understanding of key features and aspects, and to help you to address the particular requirements of examination questions so you can obtain the best possible grade.

Note that teachers and examiners are seeking evidence of an informed personal response to the text above all else. A guide such as this can help you understand the text and form your own opinions, and it can suggest areas to think about, but it cannot replace your own ideas and responses as an informed and autonomous reader.

Line references in this guide refer to the 2002 Arden Shakespeare edition of the text.

How to make the most of this guide

You may find it useful to read sections of this guide when you need them, rather than reading them from start to finish. For example, you may find it helpful to read the 'Contexts' section before you start reading the text, or to read the 'Scene summaries and commentaries' section in conjunction with the text — whether to back up your reading of it at school or college, or to help you revise. The sections relating to the Assessment Objectives will be especially useful in the weeks leading up to the exam.

Key elements

This guide is designed to help you raise your achievement in your examination response to *Othello*. It is intended for you to use throughout your AS/A-level English literature course. It will help you when you are studying the play for the first time and also during your revision.

The following features have been used throughout this guide to help you focus your understanding of the play:

Context

Context boxes give contextual evidence that relates directly to particular aspects of the text.

Build critical skills

Broaden your thinking about the text by answering questions in the **Build critical skills** boxes. These help you to consider your own opinions in order to develop your skills of criticism and analysis.

CRITICAL VIEW

Critical view boxes highlight a particular critical viewpoint that is relevant to an aspect of the main text. This allows you to develop the higher-level skills needed to come up with your own interpretation of a text.

TASK

Tasks are short and focused. They allow you to engage directly with a particular aspect of the text.

Taking it further ▶

Taking it further boxes suggest and provide further background or illuminating parallels to the text.

Top ten quotation

Follow up each cross-reference to a Top ten quotation (see pages 99–102 of this guide), where each quotation is accompanied by a commentary that shows why it is important.

Top ten quotation

Introduction

Othello is a wonderful play to study, demonstrating as it does many aspects of dramatic tragedy. Shakespeare wrote the play around 1603, giving it the full title of *The Tragedy of Othello, the Moor of Venice*. The play is a fine example of how tragedy works as a dramatic form, and you are likely to consider it closely from this perspective. *Othello* is widely viewed as a domestic tragedy between a husband and wife – one that is principally born out of jealousy. Although there is a wider conflict between the Venetians and Turks happening as part of the backdrop, the unfolding tragedy remains tightly focused on two families.

Within the play, the character of Othello can be viewed as a classic tragic hero, one who foolishly continues to believe he is right almost to the end of the play. His wife, Desdemona, is an innocent, tragic victim who, like her husband Othello, is caught in Iago's web. Many other characters become embroiled in the events that follow, which leads to their downfall as well.

The play is often considered a work that examines issues of race and ethnicity. Viewed through this critical lens, one of the reasons the tragedy occurs is because Othello is an 'outsider' operating in Venetian society. It is also seen as a study of manipulation and deceit, which principally arises from the evil and unscrupulous ways of Iago. Unlike other tragedies by Shakespeare, the play focuses on three central characters and there is an absence of a separate sub-plot. This may be what makes the tragedy here so intense.

As well as understanding *Othello* as a tragedy, you will need to consider factors such as how Shakespeare constructs his characters and how he develops particular tragic themes, and how this may represent and reflect the contextual conditions of production and reception during Shakespeare's time. It is also worth considering how the play has been presented on stage, in film and on television over the years. For example, Laurence Olivier's and Maggie Smith's performances in the 1965 film of the National Theatre production; Laurence Fishburne as the first black man to play Othello on film in Oliver Parker's 1995 film, or the Royal Shakespeare Company's 2015 production, which cast a black Iago alongside a black Othello.

Othello (called 'the Moor') is a renowned general of North African descent in the service of Venice, a proud and wealthy city-state in north-eastern Italy. He has served Venice loyally, but as the play opens there is a crisis. He has secretly married Desdemona, the only child of Brabantio, a highly respected Venetian senator. This secret act initiates the tragic pattern in the play. Iago, Othello's ancient ('ensign' or 'standard bearer') persuades Roderigo, a wealthy and gullible fool, to inform Brabantio of his daughter's shocking elopement. This elopement initiates the chaos resulting from the change in the normal order of things, that daughters should consult their fathers on who they marry.

Othello is called before the Senate by Brabantio to explain to the Duke why he has married Desdemona. He is accused of using witchcraft to seduce her, but Desdemona declares her love for and loyalty to Othello. Brabantio disowns her and warns Othello that as she deceived him, she may deceive Othello. Desdemona begs to accompany Othello on a dangerous mission: he has been appointed governor of the Mediterranean island of Cyprus, part of the Venetian empire, and must leave immediately to defend it from the Turks.

From Iago's perspective, Othello has gone against the natural order of things by appointing Michael Cassio as his lieutenant. In doing so, he has passed over the more experienced but socially inferior Iago, which throws Iago into a jealous hatred of Othello and Cassio. Iago has also heard rumours that Othello once slept with his wife, Emilia, which exacerbates his jealousy of Othello. Othello seemingly favoured Cassio because he acted as a go-between in Othello's wooing of Desdemona. Cassio is a less-experienced warrior and more of a tactician. Othello requests that Emilia should travel to Cyprus to be Desdemona's maid, and that Iago should take care of Desdemona, following Othello on a separate ship, for the difficult sea voyage.

Act 2 is set in Cyprus. Roderigo arrives there still believing he is in love with Desdemona. Iago encourages him (in return for jewels, which Roderigo thinks Iago gives to her) to believe that she will tire of Othello and turn to him. A storm delays Othello's arrival but conveniently destroys the Turkish fleet.

After an evening of celebrating this victory over the Turks, Cassio is placed in charge of the night watch while the newly-weds retire. Iago schemes to discredit Cassio. Knowing Cassio cannot hold his drink, Iago persuades him to drink heavily and induces Roderigo to provoke him, saying that he is a rival for Desdemona. Cassio strikes Roderigo and wounds Montano, the respected previous Governor of Cyprus. Hearing Iago's account, Othello dismisses Cassio immediately. Iago then manipulates Cassio for his own ends, urging him to ask Desdemona to help him win back Othello's trust and his former position. Desdemona innocently speaks to Othello on Cassio's behalf, not knowing that

Iago has hinted to Othello that Cassio's visit to Desdemona was to seduce her. Iago instructs Emilia to obtain Desdemona's cherished handkerchief, which was a gift from Othello. When she does so, Iago lies to Othello, telling him that Desdemona gave it to Cassio as a love token.

In the crucial central scenes of the play, Act 3, Scene 3 to Act 4, Scene1, Iago relentlessly works on Othello, manipulating his fears to kindle his jealousy and undermine his self-confidence. Othello demands proof of Desdemona's betrayal (which Iago has already arranged in the form of the handkerchief). The two men kneel together in a grotesque parody of a wedding, swearing a bond of loyalty to each other and pledging that they will kill Cassio and Desdemona together. Finally, as if the internal torment is too great, Othello falls into an epileptic fit.

Cassio has actually been consorting with Bianca, a Venetian courtesan (or high-class escort), and he asks her to make him a copy of a handkerchief he has found in his bedroom (where Emilia planted it). In the following scene, Bianca returns the handkerchief to Cassio while Othello watches unobserved, apparently providing proof of Iago's accusations. Othello is witnessed striking Desdemona by the shocked Lodovico, an emissary (representative) from Venice who is Desdemona's relative. By Iago's manipulative behaviour, tragic chaos starts to dominate.

Questioned by Othello, Emilia denies that Cassio has been meeting Desdemona, but he does not believe her, nor will he believe Desdemona when she protests her innocence and fidelity. In the final scene of Act 4, Emilia helps prepare Desdemona for bed to wait for Othello.

Act 5 opens with the attempted assassination of Cassio, which Othello and Iago plotted by having Iago manipulate Roderigo into attempting to kill him. This goes horribly wrong and Iago has to stab Roderigo. Here the audience sees how tragic events embroil all the characters. Although Roderigo dies, he incriminates Iago with his dying words and Cassio becomes the first to recognise Iago's malice and duplicity.

Meanwhile, the dramatic final scene is unfolding: Othello comes to the sleeping Desdemona and informs her that he will kill her. She protests her innocence, but Othello smothers her. Emilia enters, and learns for the first time the treacherous role of her husband Iago in the false accusations made against Desdemona (and her own unwitting part by securing the handkerchief). As she tries to explain the truth to Othello, Iago enters, kills her and runs off. Othello is prevented from killing Iago by Montano, and as the details of the plot are revealed to the remaining characters, Othello falls on his own sword to die as a soldier rather than be taken back to Venice in irons to be tried. Cassio is appointed governor of Cyprus and instructed to torture Iago, who although captured remains defiant and refuses to explain his actions in any way.

Target your thinking

- How does Shakespeare develop his themes and characters as the drama progresses? (**AO1**)
- In what ways does Shakespeare involve the audience in the action and create dramatic effects? (**AO2**)

Act 1, Scene 1

In Venice, Roderigo and Iago are in the middle of an argument concerning Desdemona's secret marriage to Othello. Roderigo has been paying Iago to promote his interests with Desdemona. Iago explains that he has been passed over as lieutenant to the Moor in favour of the inexperienced Cassio. He assures Roderigo that he hates Othello and only continues to serve him for his own ends. They wake up Brabantio to tell him that his daughter has eloped with Othello. When he is finally convinced that the previously rejected suitor, Roderigo, is telling the truth, Brabantio orders an armed search to arrest Othello. In the meantime Iago has slipped away to warn Othello.

Commentary The tragic nature of the plot is set up in this scene. Deception and trickery usually lead to a bad end. Othello's name is not used at all in this scene, although what is spoken is all about him. This is purposeful on Shakespeare's part and the anti-Othello language serves as a pattern for the rest of the play, whereby negatives dominate over positives. Othello's ethnicity and identity are described in negative and racist ways, already giving the audience a position on how to view Othello. Othello is presented as a stereotypical, lustful Moor. For tragedy to occur, there must be a change in the order of some kind, and this happens when there is a 'gross revolt' from nature when Desdemona chooses Othello as her husband. Iago is set up as a tragic villain. His first words are blasphemous, and the Venice he alludes to is seen as a place of corruption, conflict and disturbance. He does, of course, further this disruption by his own actions later in the play. Iago shows himself to be in possession of a lot of knowledge about Othello's movements. He is in danger of losing his main source of income, his 'purse' Roderigo, by this marriage, and must therefore do something about it.

Context

The tragic context is established here by the collision of two different ethnicities, which in the period of the play's construction, was considered as going against the natural order.

Build critical skills

At these early points in the tragedy, what impression have you formed of Iago? What impression do you have of Othello, who has not yet appeared on stage?

Other key words are introduced – service, honest, seeming, poison and devil – as well as farmyard animal images ('an old black ram is tupping your white ewe', 'your daughter and the Moor are now making the beast with two backs'). The problem of Cassio's 'fair wife' (see line 20, 'almost damned in a fair wife' and 5.1.19–20) has troubled editors, one view being that it should read 'fair life'. It could also mean what it says; Cassio has a beautiful wife who is living in the Venetian garrison with him, and is therefore known to the lascivious and envious Iago, and Iago is expressing his belief that men who marry beautiful women are damned because they will inevitably be cuckolded (an interesting precept for tragedy). Iago does not reveal himself to Brabantio (the scene takes place at night-time, and the characters are often presented as hooded or masked), and this is the beginning of him using others for his own ends while covering himself. Iago's key statement: **'I am not what I am'** (line 64), ironically echoes God's words to Moses in Exodus: 'I am that I am'. As the scene takes place in darkness, with a call for light at the end of it, this transition indicates a showing forth of truth. The two characters outside also parallel the contemporary practice of *charivari* (a French folk custom) – noise made outside a couple's house on the wedding night to show disapproval of the marriage. Their elopement characterises Othello and Desdemona as romantic but by overturning the order of things, they are potentially tragic too.

Top ten quotation

▲ Clarke Peters as Othello, Dominic West as Iago and Lily James as Desdemona at the Crucible Theatre, Sheffield, September 2011

Act 1, Scene 2

Iago claims, doubly false, that he wanted to defend Othello against Brabantio's slanders, but is not evil enough to commit murder. He tries to stir up enmity between Othello and his father-in-law, but Othello is confident that he can 'out-tongue his complaints' and he asserts his noble lineage. Cassio and the Duke's servants find Othello first and request his presence at the Senate, followed immediately by Brabantio's followers, including Roderigo. Brabantio accuses Othello of having bewitched Desdemona. They all go to the Senate for Othello to answer the case against him.

Commentary At this stage Othello does not allow himself to be provoked by Iago, who is forced into the position of onlooker when the others arrive. This is the first time the audience meets Othello and contrary to what has been said about this tragic hero before, we find that in fact, he is intelligent, erudite and poetic in his speech – embodied in his response to Brabantio's men when he says to them: 'Keep up your bright swords, for the dew will rust them' (line 59). We also note his diplomacy when he says to Brabantio that 'you shall more command with years rather than with your weapons' (line 60). The tragic theme of division is introduced with the word 'divorce'. The theme of a wider tragedy of battle between Venice and the Turks is echoed here by the two Venetian armies meeting in the street, one with the intention of fighting. Cassio is presumably lying when he tells Iago he knows nothing of the marriage as he has been the go-between throughout the courtship. The final couplet in this scene summarises the fear and prejudice in Venice against Moors and Barbarians: 'Bondslaves and pagans' who threaten to reverse the natural order.

> **Build critical skills**
>
> What is your impression of Brabantio at this point? Is he hot-headed or does he have a legitimate case?

> **Context**
>
> `Othello is obviously a respected, high-status character who the Senate call upon when there is trouble. In tragedy, his high status means he can 'fall' further than most.`

> **Context**
>
> `The wider context here is between the Christian world order of Venice and the Islamic world of Turkey and North Africa. Anyone with non-Christian background was labelled a 'pagan'. Othello is an unusual character in that he is able to straddle both worlds, yet this also puts him in a dangerous and possibly tragic position.`

Act 1, Scene 3

Brabantio publicly repeats his accusation of witchcraft against Othello, who responds by telling the story of their courtship and how Desdemona was wooed by pity and fascination for his suffering and exotic travels. In this sense, the audience can see the attraction: Othello represents African exotica. When Desdemona arrives and is asked to verify his story, she chooses her husband over her father and Brabantio disowns her despite the Duke's plea for mercy. Because Desdemona is now an outcast, and because she wants to travel

TASK

What is your impression of Iago when he speaks his soliloquy here? How do soliloquies like this increase our understanding of the tragedy?

with Othello, they both beg the Duke to allow her to accompany Othello on his mission to Cyprus. It is agreed that Desdemona will follow Othello the next morning under Iago's protection, and with Iago's wife Emilia as her maid. Brabantio's last words are a threat to Othello that Desdemona will deceive him too. This might be seen as a portent to the tragedy that follows. When Roderigo and Iago are left alone, Roderigo threatens that he will drown himself because he has lost Desdemona, but Iago quickly convinces him that if he accompanies the party to Cyprus, with plenty of money at his disposal, Desdemona will turn to him when she tires of the 'erring barbarian'. In his soliloquy Iago reveals his suspicion that Othello may have slept with Emilia, and his plan to get the lieutenancy by making Othello think Cassio is having an affair with Desdemona. Thus the audience gains insight into Iago's tragic villainy and motivation for revenge.

Commentary The streams of messengers to the Duke demonstrate the urgency of the crisis and indispensability of the 'valiant Moor'. The confusions, doubts and contradictions of the messages show the impossibility of distinguishing truth from the deception of the 'false gaze'. 'Error', 'judgement', 'reason', 'proof' and 'test' are all words used by the Duke, which prefigure Othello's situation later on in discerning the truth about his wife. Othello's speeches to the state reveal his nobility and high status: they are filled with rhetorical devices, poetic imagery, strong rhythms and the characteristics of varnished tales. The question of whether he is deliberately self-dramatising or using high-flown language has been debated by some critics, but the effect is to show him at the top of his game. He is articulate, gentle and in control of his own destiny. His speeches here should be compared with those later on when he loses control. This is, in any case, a trial scene, with Othello as the eloquent defendant and Brabantio as the aggrieved prosecutor.

Mention of monsters and cannibals is relevant to various themes in the tragedy, as is the idea that words, lies, tales and fictions can form a captivating web, evoke overwhelming emotion, and eventually lead to death and destruction. Othello and his wife must say farewell to peace and Venice, home and father; division has entered their lives and 'haste', 'speed' and 'time' must be obeyed; love has been subjugated to a call to arms. Iago's run of luck has begun but death is already being mentioned. This sense of foreboding underpins everything here.

Contempt for women, noble virtues that include love, and a habit of comparing humans to animals are evident in Iago's manipulation of Roderigo, the stereotypical unrequited lover. Like other Machiavels (unscrupulous political manipulators), Iago makes it clear he believes in free will, not destiny, and that life is what you make it. His speech in lines 331–67 contains ten injunctions to Roderigo to put money in his purse, but Roderigo is unaware of this effective technique of subliminal brainwashing. One of Roderigo's roles is to make Iago reveal his theories and practices so that an audience can be impressed by his cunning strategies, and be prepared for his later conquests.

The theme of reputation is evident in this scene in the tragedy, which is a concern for all of the characters. It is composed in blank verse, couplets and prose, and each change signifies a change of mood or dramatic effect. The structure is paralleled in many other scenes, that is, private conversations becoming public debate, and ending with a soliloquy by Iago. This always gives the impression that Iago is controlling events on all levels (as a kind of puppet-master), that he is the only character who can connect the private and the public, and that he is omnipresent.

Act 2, Scene 1

Cassio arrives at Cyprus first, then Iago and Desdemona, and finally Othello. They have been held up by a terrible storm, which has conveniently destroyed the Turkish fleet. Cassio provokes Iago when he courteously kisses Emilia and patronises Iago as being only a soldier and not a scholar. Iago persuades Roderigo that Cassio must be 'displanted' as he stands in the way of Roderigo's chances of Desdemona turning to him when she inevitably tires of Othello. Iago's soliloquy here states his plan to avenge himself on both Othello and Cassio, who he suspects to have cuckolded him as well.

Taking it further ▶

Compare two different performances of Iago's conversation with Roderigo and his subsequent soliloquy, which tells of his plan to ruin Othello and Cassio. Think about the ways in which aspects of setting and staging bring the tragedy to life. Which performance do you prefer and why?

Commentary Storms are used in literature to represent disruption of the normal order of things and to prefigure disaster. The division of Othello from his wife and his lieutenant also prefigure the emotional divisions that follow in the tragedy. The external Turkish threat is replaced by that of the 'Turk' within Iago, which is harder to deal with because it is invisible. Anxiety and tension are created by Shakespeare via the delayed arrivals and fear of Othello's demise. Dramatic arrivals and uncertainty are continuing features here that were first established in Act 1. Ironically, but fittingly, the salvo to announce Othello's arrival is mistakenly given for Iago instead, who had made 'most favourable and happy speed'; he had overtaken Othello, whose ship left many hours before his and arrived a week earlier than expected, as if favoured by the gods. This indicates a change in status in the tragedy; Iago is now in control of events. Cassio offers a 'Hail Mary' to the 'divine Desdemona', uttering hyperbolic flattery of a traditional courtly kind. She indulges in banter with Iago to hide her anxiety about Othello's safety, thus being guilty of putting on an act. Her apparent flirtation with Cassio confirms Iago's claim to Roderigo that he is her 'second choice' and therefore Cassio must be removed. Wearing a metaphorical clown's mask, Iago unfairly criticises his wife for talking too much and gives vent to his own misogyny, calling women 'wild cats, devils'. The tragic theme of speech, tongue, words and slander is further reinforced here, and 'Alas, she has no speech' (line 103) previews Desdemona's and Emilia's tragic ends. Iago's aside to the audience forces us to see others the way he sees them, as naive and foolish, and we are impressed by his powers of improvisation. His description of Cassio as 'a slipper and subtle knave, a finder out of occasions' (line 239) and 'a devilish knave' (line 242) actually apply to himself, and indicate how Iago sees everyone in his own image. The scene drastically ramps up the possibilities of events evolving into tragedy.

Act 2, Scene 2

A herald declares that Othello has granted an evening of celebration for the destruction of the Turkish fleet and for his own marriage.

Commentary This is a very brief scene, which shortcuts the need to explain the celebratory context for Act 2, Scene 3. In terms of the tragedy, it is ominous that a celebration over a marriage is closely linked to success in war.

Act 2, Scene 3

Cassio is put in charge of the watch while Othello and Desdemona retire. Iago tricks Cassio into drinking to the point of drunkenness and Roderigo provokes him according to plan, immediately confirming Iago's slanderous prediction of Cassio's uncontrolled behaviour to the governor, Montano. Cassio strikes Roderigo and wounds Montano, who has intervened to stop the fight. Othello is roused from bed and to anger. He dismisses Cassio from his service after hearing Iago's cunning account of the incident. Cassio appeals to Iago for advice regarding the loss of his reputation and denounces the demon drink. Iago plays the good friend and tells him to use Desdemona to try to get his place back since the 'General's wife' is now 'the General' (line 310).

Commentary Iago's description of Desdemona is low and coarse, contrasting with the flattering and courteous comments that Cassio makes about her. Iago has set up revellers to trap Cassio into having to be sociable, and to drink the health of 'black Othello' or prove himself ill-mannered. Thus Iago uses virtues as well as faults against their owners to unmake what has been made: the lieutenancy, the marital union, and the respect of Cypriots for Venetians. In Iago's view, real men can hold their drink and be the life and soul of the party, as he can. Drunkenness was seen as a state akin to bestiality, since it involves loss of clear vision and reason, and is an 'enemy in their mouths to steal away their brains' (line 286).

Iago manages the action, entrances and exits, and the timing of this scene in a masterly fashion, and comes out of it well himself. He diminishes people's reputations, both in their eyes and in the view of others, and raises himself in everyone's esteem. Whenever Iago can get in a reference to sex, he does so, as in the 'bride and groom/Divesting them for bed' (lines 176–7), and his speech equates love with 'opposition bloody' and the battle imagery of 'swords', 'tilting', 'odds' and 'action.' Speech and the disadvantages of those who cannot speak (Cassio and Montano), are made clear in this scene. Double-talking Iago can speak in a way that both condemns Cassio and yet appears to be pleading on his behalf, as a loyal friend would. It is of crucial significance that Othello says, 'My blood begins my safer guides to rule,/And passion, having my best judgement collied,/Always to lead the way' (lines 201–2). This is tantamount to having fallen; to letting passion overrule the safer guide of judgement, as in Adam's original sin. To reinforce a recurring image, 'collied' means 'blackened'. Othello never recovers from his giving way to the deadly sin of wrath at this moment.

The dismissal of Cassio without having heard his statement could be considered hasty and the punishment extreme: 'never more be officer of mine' (line 245), especially for a close friend (called Michael) as well as a recently appointed officer. Using a military punishment against Cassio, partly because he disturbed Desdemona's rest, demonstrates Othello's inability to keep the private and the public separate, though he promised the Senate he would be able to do so. The broken bond between Othello and Cassio (who is his link with Desdemona and respectable society) is the beginning of the end of Othello's reputation and of his marriage. He is now caught in a tragic spiral heading downwards. From then on Iago takes the place of Cassio. Iago once again shows expert knowledge of character, accurately predicting that Othello will overreact to the brawl and that Desdemona will exceed their brief and hold it in a vice 'not to do more than she is requested'.

Act 3, Scene 1

After a sleepless night, Cassio brings musicians to play music for the awakening of the couple, but they are dismissed by Othello. Cassio tells Iago that he has asked Emilia to arrange for him to see Desdemona. Emilia tells Cassio that she has overheard Othello say that Cassio will have to wait a while for the sake of decency, but he will be restored to his place at the first opportunity. However Cassio still insists on speaking to Desdemona alone.

Commentary This brief and apparently redundant scene actually serves to reinforce Cassio's rejection by Othello, who ominously dismisses the musicians hired by Cassio as a celebration of the consummation. It is another example of how bedroom intimacy between Othello and Desdemona is disturbed by external noise, an invasion of the private by the public, and love by war, because Othello goes off to inspect fortifications instead. Since an appreciation of gentle music was considered to be a noble and civilising attribute, it may be significant that Othello does not care for it, preferring instead the trumpeting of war. This may symbolise his 'dis-enobling' in the tragic pattern at work.

TASK
The moral atmosphere of Cyprus differs to the austerity of the Duke's court in Venice. In what ways do the characters behave and feel differently in this new setting? Why do you think Shakespeare chose to violate the classical unity of place by moving his tragedy to Cyprus?

Context

The pause in tragic events here — via the musicians and the Clown — may give the audience a breather from the intensity of the action so far. Clowns (or fools) are often used by Shakespeare to expose the frailties and true condition of characters within tragedy.

9

TASK

It may not surprise you that Act 3, Scene 1, or certain parts of it, are cut or curtailed from many modern productions of *Othello*. Why do you think this might be the case?

Act 3, Scene 2

Othello does his job of attending to the fortification of the island of Cyprus.

Commentary This creates an ironic counterpoint to his personal invasion by the enemy in the scene that comes next.

Act 3, Scene 3

Desdemona assures Cassio, with Emilia as a witness, that she will pursue his cause. Iago points out to Othello Cassio's hasty departure on their arrival. Desdemona starts to pressure Othello into seeing Cassio in order to reinstate him. He gives way to her but then tells her to leave him. Iago cleverly introduces to Othello the idea of his wife's infidelity with Cassio. As a result, Othello asks Iago to get Emilia to spy on Desdemona. When Desdemona returns, he complains of a headache and she produces a handkerchief to bind it, but drops it unnoticed. Emilia picks it up and gives it to Iago, who had previously asked for it, and now conceives of a use for it. Othello returns alone to continue the dialogue with Iago. He is tortured by visions of Desdemona with Cassio and makes a highly elaborate farewell to war and the old Othello. He demands proof from Iago to confirm his distrust. Iago tells him that Cassio revealed his intimacy with Desdemona in a dream heard by himself, and then mentions that Cassio has Desdemona's handkerchief, which was given to her by Othello. Othello then summons the evil spirits of 'black vengeance' and allies himself to his new lieutenant, Iago, who swears loyalty to 'wronged Othello's service' and vows to kill Cassio if Othello will kill Desdemona.

Commentary Shakespeare has to keep up the relentless pace to remove any opportunity for questions to creep into Othello's mind, or for him to meet Cassio and Desdemona during this onslaught. This is known to some critics as the temptation or corruption scene. The temptation, as with the apple in Eden, is of forbidden knowledge; Iago knows something that Othello does not, which drives him mad, first with curiosity and then with doubt. Othello cannot bear to 'know't a little' and becomes obsessed with the need to know more, which was Eve's original 'tragic' sin.

Iago is lucky to find himself alone with Othello at this key moment, which may be attributed to Desdemona having gone too far in her insistent demands on Cassio's behalf and his needing a bit of peace. Again, this suggests the tragic division between them. Desdemona aids Iago's case by being excessive, and therefore arousing suspicion. She also criticises Othello for 'mammering on' (line 70), and makes an unfortunate connection between Cassio and wooing by using the ambiguous word 'suitor'. Othello also paves the way for Iago's assault by saying that without Desdemona's love 'Chaos is come again' (line 92).

Iago dominates the dialogue by controlling its content through having more lines and by imposing his animal diction. He has won the battle between the orators;

Othello's speeches have not only become short but repetitive, grammatically incomplete and highly exclamatory – even inarticulate. The word 'satisfaction' is used several times in this scene by Iago, who gives it a sexual connotation as well as the meaning of satisfying curiosity with knowledge; he taunts Othello with it in both senses. Othello and Iago share lines as well as diction throughout this scene, indicating the bond forming between them. They almost 're-marry' each other.

Much use is made by Iago of words relating to vision, working on Othello's imagination and a need for 'ocular proof'. Othello sets up his own imprisoning process of thinking and acting when he avows: 'I'll see before I doubt; when I doubt, prove/And on the proof... Away at once with love or jealousy!' (lines 193–5). This may seem reasonable, but it excludes the essential stage in the pursuit of truth of speaking to the accused to check if there is another point of view or explanation. There is also the logistical problem of proving this; one can prove adultery but not fidelity, and there is no one to present the case for the defence. Othello seems more bothered by the shared possession of Desdemona, which damages his public honour, than by the hurt of private betrayal (lines 271–2). Once evil spirits are conjured, the process can no more be reversed than the 'compulsive course' of the sea with which Othello again identifies himself (lines 456–7). This sense of compulsion is important to note as the tragedy now seems fixed and inevitable.

Context

```
Initially, comedies and tragedies had the same structure.
In the first instance, there is an 'old' world that exists.
This 'old' world is given some kind of disruption – often
a relationship shift or change. Comedies and tragedies
then enter a 'chaotic' and 'disrupted' phase (usually
at the centre of the play), of which Act 3, Scene 3
is typical. In comedies this is resolved and forms a
'new' world. In tragedies, this is not resolved and the
'disrupted' phase continues, resulting in death. The 'new'
world can only begin after the deaths of the central
characters.
```

TASK

During this scene an extraordinary transformation takes place, and Othello and Iago have become conspirators in a double murder plot. Othello is no longer noble. Can this be attributed to Iago's manipulative skills alone or are there some weaknesses in Othello that he is exploiting?

At this central point in the tragedy, Othello starts to become Iago, sharing his farmyard view of sex and his misogyny. The visual effect of Othello and Iago kneeling is strikingly symbolic of how Othello has been brought 'low' by Iago. Their ritual oath is a sealing of a contract with the devil: 'I am your own forever' says Iago (line 481), taking possession of Othello in a travesty of a wedding ceremony. Desdemona has been replaced as Othello's soulmate and partner by Iago the magus, master, teacher and adviser. Othello becomes his dependent slave, playing the female role to Iago in the same way as Cassio and Roderigo are forced to because of his apparent superior knowledge. Iago would not have asked for the handkerchief 'a hundred times' unless he wanted it in case an opportunity to make malicious use of it presented itself. Iago knows what is precious to others and how he can gain power over them through what they value.

▲ Othello and Iago kneeling to pledge their plot to kill Desdemona: Eamonn Walker as Othello and Tim Mcinnerny as Iago at Shakespeare's Globe, London, 2007

There is a big question about how much Emilia realises about her husband's true character and his intentions with the handkerchief. That she tries to please him, even at the expense of upsetting her mistress, and though he treats her contemptuously, reflects the subordinate position of women at this time. Claiming that Cassio's cashiering grieves her husband (line 3) suggests that she is, in fact, fooled by him and that he misleads her about his real attributes to others. When Iago dismisses his wife in line 324, it echoes Othello's dismissal of Desdemona at the beginning of the scene and brings the two marriages into parallel. Othello is already too firmly in Iago's clutches to ever regain his former position, and only asks for proof when a doubt has already been established. In this state of mind all future apparent evidence will be twisted to fit the hypothesis until it becomes a certainty. The headache is symbolic of Othello having accepted Iago's offer of the part of the cuckold, visually represented by horns. One of many ironies in this scene and one that hangs over the rest of the play, is that the loss of the handkerchief is caused not by Desdemona but by Othello himself, who pushes it away as a rejection of her love and concern. Clearly Othello's mental instability at this point demonstrates that he is heading for tragedy.

Act 3, Scene 4

Desdemona sends the Clown to fetch Cassio. She laments to Emilia on the loss of her handkerchief. Othello arrives and asks to see it, telling her that it is a magic handkerchief. Desdemona lies about its whereabouts and counters his demands for her to produce it with her own insistence that he reinstate Cassio. Othello walks out in a rage as Iago and Cassio enter. Cassio wants to know without further delay whether he will be readmitted into Othello's service. Desdemona admits that Othello is not himself, which she blames on state matters, though Emilia is unconvinced. A courtesan, Bianca, complains to Cassio about his neglect of her, and he asks her to copy the handkerchief, which he has found in his bedroom.

Commentary There is a breakdown of communication between Othello and Desdemona, and a revelation of the lack of understanding they have of each other's character. Lying in both senses has become a dominant theme and seems to be catching. Desdemona responds like a scared child to Othello's demand, with non-committal and frightened answers and attempts to change the subject. The tale about the handkerchief may be another of Othello's romantic and dramatic fictions. His apparent belief in its magic, however, shows a pagan belief in the supernatural, at odds with the other Othello of Act 1, with his respect for reason, and suggests that his hidden past may be surfacing. We know that he knows she hasn't got the handkerchief, and we see his bullying as bordering on sadistic torture, on par with Iago's behaviour.

We see the contrast between the worldly Emilia, who has had experience of marriage, men and their jealousy, and her naive mistress. Cassio's insistence on knowing about his reinstatement reinforces the idea that not knowing is painful, and he is extreme in his demand and careless of the cost to Desdemona. He speaks formally and respectfully to Desdemona, who can aid him, but disrespectfully to Bianca, with whom he satisfies his sexual appetites after dark. It is deceitful of him to not want Othello to see him 'womaned'. Like the two other men, he dismisses his woman and asks to be left alone. Telling Bianca, 'Not that I love you not' (line 197) has the devious circumlocution of an Iago utterance, and in this scene the audience starts to wonder whether Cassio is really so different from Iago beneath his gentlemanly manners and exterior. Emilia's lie, 'I know not, madam' (line 24), is a crucial thematic utterance in the play, and the last point at which the tragedy could be averted by the truth.

Act 4, Scene 1

Iago continues where he left off in Act 3, Scene 3, forcing Othello to discuss the handkerchief and Desdemona's honesty. He claims that Cassio has admitted the affair to him, provoking Othello to fall into a fit. Cassio appears during it but Iago gets rid of him quickly. When Cassio returns, it is to be an unwitting performer in a charade engineered by Iago, with Othello as spectator, whereby Bianca is substituted for Desdemona as the topic of conversation. Bianca appears in person at this point and throws back the handkerchief in the sight of Othello. Cassio chases after her, which gives Iago the opportunity to move Othello on the point of settling that Desdemona and Cassio will die the same evening. Officials from Venice, relatives of Desdemona, arrive with a letter for Othello, and he strikes her in front of them. The shocked Lodovico is told by Iago that this is typical of Othello's current behaviour.

Commentary This is the best example of 'seeing is believing' in the tragedy. Iago is firmly in control in this scene, and of its play within a play created by himself. He initiates and directs the action and reactions, timings of entrances and exits, and the pat delivery of lines with attendant body language. Othello has now been reduced to a common spy, and one who falsely interprets what he sees. He has fallen so low as to be writhing on the ground, with triumphant Iago looking down on him and sadistically enjoying this de-creation of the great general.

Othello's speech, or rather raving rant (lines 35–44) is full of questions and exclamation marks, obsessive repetition and lapses of syntax. This linguistic breakdown reflects his mental collapse, as does his falling to the ground in a fit of 'savage madness'. Noses and lips are surrogate genitalia, and once again Othello is at the mercy of his visual imagination. The scene ends in prose, another sign of Othello's tragic mental breakdown. By line 253, his speech has become even more incoherent and disjointed, and schizophrenically polarised into the private and public modes — that is the old and the new Othello.

Iago has the luck of the devil in that Bianca turns up to reject the handkerchief at the appropriate moment, unwittingly confirming Desdemona's death sentence. He even knows that Cassio can be counted upon to laugh excessively. His addressing of Cassio as 'Lieutenant' is sadistic malice. Iago calls Bianca a 'bauble' and the audience sees more of his double standards regarding women. Iago persuades Othello to 'strangle her in her bed' (line 204) rather than use poison. There are many possible reasons for this: it will make Othello's guilt the greater, strangulation is a military assault in which the stronger prevails; it is a travesty of the act of love to kill in bed with a pillow. The arrival of the Venetians to relieve Othello and to promote Cassio — although logical, since the Turkish threat has been temporarily removed — seems to be an indictment of Othello and a confirmation of Cassio as his replacement in love and war. Striking a woman was regarded as a cowardly and dishonourable at the time, especially in public, and this action damages both their reputations.

Taking it further ▶▶

Bianca is the third woman to become embroiled in the tragic events. These women represent three social classes and show how the tragedy permeates the whole of society. Why does Bianca reject the handkerchief? Consider her wider role: how does Bianca help Shakespeare to develop themes and ideas?

CRITICAL VIEW

In *Shakespeare: the Basics* (2000), Sean McEvoy argues that feminist critics read Othello's violent jealousy as the product of a social system where women are dominated and possessed by men. How would you respond to McEvoy's view? Use examples from the text to support your response.

Act 4, Scene 2

Othello interrogates Emilia about Desdemona's alleged meetings with Cassio. She denies them, but Othello does not believe her. Desdemona swears her innocence to Othello, again to no avail. He insults Emilia and Desdemona by giving her money as he leaves. She asks Emilia to put her wedding sheets on the bed and weeps in front of Iago about losing her lord. Roderigo demands the return of his jewellery, which Iago pretended to have given to Desdemona, and states his intention to stop his 'unlawful solicitation' of her. In return, Iago promises he will enjoy Desdemona the following night (when he knows she will be dead) if he kills Cassio.

Commentary Known sometimes as the brothel scene, this episode is an example of how evidence can only confirm a suspicion, not dislodge it. Emilia's truth seems the same as if she were telling lies. Desdemona kneels to Othello, an image of pathos, childlike venerability and subservience, and a reminder of the unholy alliance between himself and Iago. Othello seems to have fallen into self-pity at being a figure of scorn. He uses base imagery of smell, hell, weeds and reptiles/insects. Iago again tries to stop his wife's mouth in a preview of the final scene. Desdemona kneeling to Iago (line 153) is a grotesque irony and an echo. There is feasting and entertaining of the Venetians as an ironic public background to the private horror. 'Is't possible?' (line 88) is the question that haunts the play, and to which Iago provides answers on many levels. Iago, whose prior knowledge is usually accurate, says Othello is being sent to Mauretania in Africa; there would have been no military reason for the Senate to post him there – it having no connection to the Venetian empire – but there is a symbolism in him not being recalled to Venice, but to the imagined original homeland of Moors at that time, and in Desdemona's not being allowed to return home; perhaps Brabantio's influence at work, as she herself suggests. The wedding sheets are about to become winding sheets, as her bed is about to become her grave (as in *Romeo and Juliet*).

> **Context**
>
> Desdemona's reflection on her 'wretched fortune' links to another earlier concept within tragedy – the idea of the wheel of fortune. If life goes well, then the individual is at the top of the wheel. However, fate, or events in life, can easily turn the wheel's rotation so that the individual finds themselves at the bottom of the wheel, where tragedy can sometimes occur.

Act 4, Scene 3

It is night and Othello orders Desdemona to go to bed, dismiss Emilia and wait for him. As she is being prepared for bed, Desdemona sings a death song. Emilia disagrees with Desdemona that adultery could never be justified, but blames men for women's faults.

Commentary In what is sometimes referred to as the willow scene, a scene of high tension and pathos, the wives are forced into a bond of ignorance and passivity, as a contrasting parallel to that between their husbands. There is a flow of warmth and tenderness between Desdemona and Emilia, which is ironic in many different ways. Emilia has taken on the dominant role of mother figure (as Iago has 'father'd' Othello), soothing, counselling and undressing, while Desdemona, in her white nightdress, is the pious and vulnerable child at bedtime, as well as the virgin sacrifice being prepared. Desdemona thinks she is preparing for love, but is in fact preparing for her death, which is emphasised by the Gothic atmosphere – complete with superstition, a wind and a phantom – knocking on the door. The tragic song of her mother's maid, which has prophetic references to the death of a woman caused by the betrayal of a lover, is Desdemona's swan song. Perhaps her mother's maid was black, but in any case her name, **'Barbary'**, seems too coincidental not to be an oblique reference to the Berbers, or Moors, and victimisation.

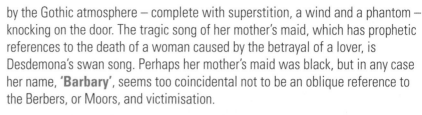

Top ten quotation

Taking it further ▶

Desdemona and Emilia discuss gender politics and marriage. How do their respective social positions and life experiences shape their beliefs? How might Shakespeare's contemporary audience have responded to their points of view? In your opinion, whose argument is stronger? How do their different points of view reinforce aspects of tragedy?

Act 5, Scene 1

In the darkness, Iago conducts Roderigo's attack on Cassio, who is returning from Bianca's house. It is Iago's intention that both men should die to prevent the truth from being revealed. Roderigo fails and instead is wounded by Cassio, who receives a leg injury from Iago before the latter exits. Othello can hear the fight and assumes Cassio has been killed as planned. After Lodivico and Gratiano have heard the cries of the two wounded, Iago re-enters bearing a light and offers to help Cassio, while also taking the opportunity to stab Roderigo. When Bianca appears, Iago points to her fright and paleness as evidence of her conspiracy in the attack on Cassio. Emilia turns up, insults Bianca, and is instructed by Iago to inform Othello and Desdemona of what has happened, though he presumably does not expect Desdemona to still be alive. Roderigo's death and Cassio's maiming show how close tragedy is now to the central characters of the play.

▲ Desdemona and Emilia discuss gender politics and marriage: Ayesha Dharker as Emilia and Joanna Vanderham as Desdemona. The Royal Shakespeare Theatre, Stratford-upon-Avon, 2015

Commentary Everyone is a villain, victim, witness or suspect in Iago's 'play'. It has been suggested that Iago starts making mistakes here, or that his run of luck has finished, though he would still be in the clear as long as Roderigo died, and once Othello has become a murderer his accusations will not carry much weight. Again Othello misinterprets the action, mistaking the voice of Roderigo for Cassio. His retiring couplet (lines 128–9) is that of the stereotypical stage villain, and exaggerated in that he is going to strangle her, not spill her blood. Roderigo's naming of Iago as an 'inhuman dog' is the first time Iago has been seen for what he is. His envy of Cassio's 'daily beauty' suggest that Cassio has been an equally prime target all along, and that Iago knows what 'beauty' is and resents being deprived of it, though he has up to now denied the existence of such an abstract and effeminate concept, along with love, honour and reputation. It is obviously ironic that Iago should be a light-bearer, and that once again he should offer support for Cassio and concern for his 'dear friend' Roderigo. He quickly turns appearance (Bianca's) into evidence, for a situation that is plausible but false. Bianca pointedly claims to be as honest as Emilia, and Iago's final couplet confirms that tragedy is about to happen. Although he has prepared things well, he also recognises the role chance has to play.

Act 5, Scene 2

Othello enters the bedroom and kisses the sleeping Desdemona while justifying what he intends to do. She wakes and he warns her that he is about to kill her so she had better say her prayers. She asks that Cassio be sent for to testify on her behalf, but is told that he is dead. She begs for more time but Othello refuses and smothers her. Emilia arrives too late to prevent Desdemona's death but in time to hear Desdemona's claim it was not Othello's fault. Emilia is thunderstruck to be told by Othello that 'honest, honest Iago' was the person who claimed Desdemona was false. She rails at Othello for his ignorance and stupidity, and also verbally attacks her husband when he confirms the slander, despite his ordering her to be quiet. Gratiano then delivers the news that Brabantio is dead.

When Emilia explains how Cassio got the handkerchief, Othello tries to kill Iago but is disarmed, and Iago gets the opportunity to kill Emilia and run away. Montano chases Iago while Gratiano keeps guard outside the bedroom door. Emilia dies singing the 'Willow Song' and vouching for Desdemona's love for the 'cruel Moor'. Othello finds another sword and calls Gratiano in to witness his speech of self-damnation, an audience then swelled by Lodovico, Cassio, Montano and Iago. Iago refuses to satisfy Othello's need to know the cause of his hatred. Written evidence is produced against Iago from the dead Roderigo's pockets. Cassio is to be governor in Cyprus. Iago is to be tortured by him, and Othello is to be taken back to Venice for trial, but prevents this by killing himself in military fashion. He falls upon the bed with the bodies of Desdemona and Emilia. The tragedy is complete.

Commentary Samuel Johnson found the tragedy of this scene to be so moving as to be unendurable, and another critic called it 'unutterable agony'; it has been said that it pushes the limits of what can be shown on stage. As we might expect at the end of a tragedy, 'Chaos is come again', with much light/dark imagery to emphasise this. With the announcement that 'yonder foul murder's done' (line 105), the public and private, war and love, Christian and Turk are subsumed into each other as tragic disorder reigns. Othello takes on the role of Desdemona's protector and when he asks her if she has said her prayers he appears a travesty of parental concern. Desdemona waits for him like a little girl, to be tucked up and kissed goodnight, yet she is doubly betrayed by him – her husband and father figure. We have not seen him for a while and he has a semblance of calm, which proves to be false: Desdemona comments on his gnawing of his lip, his rolling eyes and 'bloody passion', and he is overcome with wrath when she weeps for Cassio's supposed murder. Emilia is forthright in her condemnation of Othello's act and her racism emerges in the language of 'dirt'. It is her tragedy as well as Othello's and Desdemona's; she made a mistake, sees a loved one dead and ends by bravely defying slander and conspiracy at the cost of her life.

A key piece of minor information comes when Gratiano delivers the news that Brabantio is dead. There is almost no reaction from the characters at this point, but

Top ten quotation

Top ten quotation

the announcement of his death reinforces several aspects of the tragedy. First of all, his last speech has been apparently confirmed by events; second, his death is part of the wider collapse and chaos of Venetian society; and finally, Desdemona has now lost her father figure, the only one who actually tried to protect her.

Othello's claim to be protecting other men by killing Desdemona (cf. the 'Willow Song's' 'You'll couch with moe [sic] men') is either self-delusion or an indication that he, like Iago, now sees this as a gender war. His forcing her down on the bed, lying on top of her, and silencing her in a breathless spasm is a horrible travesty of the consummation of the previous night. (The word 'die' was used then as a form of orgasm.) It is an un-Christian act that jeopardises both their souls; he kills her in a moment of wrath, provoked by another visual misinterpretation (her tears), and does not allow her time to pray.

Iago, who feels confident that he cannot be blamed for someone else's foolish credulity, makes the mistake of thinking he is untouchable, and that he can rely on his wife's continuing obedience to stay silent. It is fitting that he should be undone by a woman, and by his dupe Roderigo, who has convenient (albeit unlikely) letters in his pocket to convict Iago. Othello makes the appeal: 'Iago knows' in line 208, but Iago withdraws his knowledge with **'what you know, you know'** (line 300), which is nothing. The villain's refusal to speak at the end is unusual, when compared to other Shakespearean plays, and seems unnatural for a man who throughout the rest of the play has used words incredibly successfully (albeit for evil effect). He may be pushing Othello to suicide, which would guarantee Othello's damnation, which would carry his plan to conclusion and the death of the key witness would be to his own advantage. Iago's self-esteem would be damaged by any admission of envy or jealousy. Cassio's promotion at the end of the play, and being alive to see it and suffer from it, is probably the worst punishment for Iago (or is it his exclusion from the trinity of loved ones on the bed?). Fortune's wheel turns very quickly now, and a 'new' world emerges; the new governor of Cyprus is the recently dismissed lieutenant. Cassio's forgiveness and charity mark him out as the true Christian. That he is male, white and Christian restores the social order.

Lodovico calls Othello 'rash' and 'unfortunate'; the victim of a combination of impetuosity and ill fate. Othello also blames fate ('ill-starred wretch' and 'error of the moon') rather than himself. His claims to have loved **'too well'** and to be an 'honourable murderer' are self-exculpating (the latter phrase is, according to the Penguin edition notes, said with 'bitter irony', but this is debatable). Surrendering to illusions and rewriting history has been his tragic weakness, from first to last, and he may be doing it again at the end (even though he thinks he is not). He reverts to the role of a valiant Christian killing the Turk, the enemy of his adopted state who is also his inner self. The act of murdering Desdemona represents killing the better (perhaps Christian) half of himself. This means that he still has to deal with the enemy Turk, which he fails to do in his strangely unsuccessful attempts to kill the 'devil' Iago, but he does finally succeed in killing himself.

Target your thinking

- How are themes expressed through both the play's language and its action? (**AO2**)
- In what ways might contextual understanding shape your response to the play's themes? (**AO3**)
- How might different audiences from different times respond differently to some of the play's themes? (**AO5**)

Love and war

In the medieval period of chivalry, the courtly lover was a knight dedicated to a cause and devoted to his lady, whose favour he won through his military skills and dangerous quests, as well as by being handsome and attentive. In *Othello*, the three main male characters are soldiers, and the three want to be loved.

The various types of love exemplified in the play are all questionable. Brabantio's love for his daughter seems more like possessiveness. He is quick to disown and repudiate her, as dying of 'pure grief' may be a consequence of his loss of respect in Venetian society because of his daughter's 'match' and his shame at the prospect of 'filthy' progeny. Desdemona does not seem unduly worried to have lost her father's love and does not express her feelings towards him, except in one comment: 'I have lost him too' (4.2.47).

Self-love, the primary sin of pride, could be laid at Iago's door, and possibly Othello's. Roderigo is in the grip of infatuation, an obsessive but illusory form of love that can depart as quickly as it arrives, and apparently does so in his case. For Iago romantic love does not exist, being 'merely a lust of the blood' and 'a permission of the will' (1.3.335), and this seems to describe not only his marriage but also Cassio's relationship with Bianca. Iago dishonestly avows his love for Othello in the ancient and feudal traditions of dutiful affection between master and servant and brothers-in-arms. Emilia is willing to lie for her husband and die for her mistress (despite having known her for only a matter of days), but both of these forms of love seem adulterated by impure motives – self-interest and guilt respectively.

Part of the tragedy of the play may be how Othello embodies the conflict between the roles of husband and soldier, which is not a problem for Iago since he does not believe in love or respect women. Othello is the antithesis of Cassio, he is an experienced soldier but an inexperienced lover. Othello is used to the 'flinty and steel couch of war' (1.3.231), has an affinity for 'hardness', and his epithet in Act 1 is 'valiant'. He admits that he is 'little blessed with the soft phrase of peace' (1.3.83) and we never see him engaged in the gentle art of love. Only by chance encounter and Desdemona's encouragement does he become a lover during his nine months' leave in Venice; he is there and invited into ruling-class homes because of his military expertise and experiences. Othello is not an independent being, but at the mercy of and a servant to the state, to be posted according to the Senate's will. An all-male environment and a soldier's lifestyle do not easily accommodate women and domesticity. The threat of war creates a background of pressing urgency that overrules the complaint of a bereft father and pushes all personal circumstances aside, even on a husband's wedding night; the Duke tells Othello he must be 'content to slubber the gloss of your new fortunes with this more stubborn and boisterous expedition' (1.3.228–9).

The Turkish threat of war symbolises not only the dark side of Othello, which will destroy him from within, but also Iago's determination to undermine his marriage, society and the moral universe. Iago is a servant at the command of others, but unlike Othello he fights against the system and tries to prove he can defeat it through his strategic cunning and the ruthlessness of the hardened campaigner. He is the spirit of competition and violence, and he has the high ground throughout the play. He is too proud to be a suitor and despises the effete and effeminate Cassio, who cannot take his drink, talks poetic nonsense and who kisses ladies' hands. Iago comments on the unmanliness of both Othello and Cassio, and despises women generally because they are not men and cannot be soldiers. His triumph is to persuade Othello and Roderigo to think that disillusion and defeat can be turned into victorious conquest. He also tricks Roderigo into fatally exchanging the courtly lover's suit in Venice for the assassin's cloak in Cyprus.

Desdemona is new to and naive about both love and war, which for her are connected because of the idealism of her youth and the influence of romantic stories. She cannot differentiate between Othello as a husband and Othello as a soldier, not realising that she should not interfere in military matters. Neither can she seem to comprehend why Cassio cannot be immediately reinstated after his cashiering, without giving grave offence to the wounded Montano and to the Cypriots (who he is there to protect from barbarism, rather than to disturb with midnight brawls). She craves excitement and travel to compensate for her sheltered and restricted upbringing, and to feed her imagination, and is determined not to be a 'moth of peace', but these tragic desires lead her to her death.

CRITICAL VIEW

Fundamentally the tragedy is about a disastrous marriage experiment. How far do you agree?

Lieutenant Cassio is the link to the pre-play romantic and military events of the elopement and the promotion. He unites, as the uniformed lover, the comrade and the courtier, the public officer and the private womaniser. He worships the unobtainable 'divine Desdemona' but wrangles with Bianca. Cassio is the subject of many comments and conversations between the main trio of characters about his swordplay and sexual prowess. As the only real survivor of the main characters, he is both tragic victim and victor; Iago beat him but is his to torture.

Jealousy and honesty

The tragedy of *Othello* appears to be built around the twin themes of jealousy and honesty.

Jealousy

Jealousy was considered to be an aspect of the deadly sin of envy, since both involve a desire to possess. The concept of jealousy had a wider meaning then than nowadays, but was most often used to denote suspicion of one's sexual partner. However, some critics have seen the tragedy differently. According to the Russian novelist Dostoevsky, 'Othello was not jealous, he was trustful' and Coleridge said, 'I do not think there is any jealousy, properly so called, in the character of Othello'. Othello, Desdemona and Iago ('The Moor is of a free and open nature' – 1.3.398) are at pains to point out that he is not jealous, certainly he has not so far shown any disposition to be so, having used Cassio as a chaperone and go-between, and having handed Desdemona over to Iago for the voyage to Cyprus. Coleridge asserts that 'Iago's suggestions ... are quite new to him'. This may be true, and the reason they are so effective. One cannot protect oneself against something that cannot be foreseen and is outside of one's previous experience.

There are other characters who might be considered guilty of jealousy or envy. Iago is envious of Cassio having the lieutenancy, good looks and manners, and a 'daily beauty in his life', of Othello having Desdemona, and of Roderigo having money. He claims to believe that that both Othello and Cassio have slept with his wife, Emilia, and convincingly describes sexual jealousy as a gnawing of the entrails. Bianca is jealous of the owner of the handkerchief; with whom she suspects Cassio has spent the last eight days. Desdemona is envious of Othello's life of travel and excitement, and is determined to become a part of it, despite the unconventionality of her accompanying him to a war zone.

Honesty

The word 'honest' was in transition at the time *Othello* was written, according to the critic William Empson, and had several and, appropriately, almost opposite meanings. It denoted the aristocratic virtues of truthfulness, faithfulness and absence of duplicity, which is how it is mostly used in the play, but could also refer to a down-to-earth frankness and lack of pretension, which is how Iago sometimes makes ironic use of it. Its extensive usage in the play draws attention to it, and gives rise to the claim that it is honesty rather than jealousy that is the main theme. 'Honest' is used 52 times and 'honour' eight times; the two words are obviously related; without honesty, that is, without integrity, one cannot have honour, that is, respect and reputation. It is reputation that obviously makes men 'immortal' (2.3.237) and the opposite of bestial, but because it is an abstract concept dependent on words spoken about someone, it is vulnerable to slander. The noble view, expressed by Cassio, was that death was preferable to dishonour.

▲ Orson Welles directed the 1952 film version and took the part of Othello, with Suzanne Cloutier as Desdemona

Honesty and honour are obviously related.

There is evidence that Othello is more concerned about his honour than about Desdemona's fidelity. His disastrous rejection of Cassio is caused by his belief that his honour has been impugned by Cassio's wounding of Montano. Coleridge claims that 'Iago would not have succeeded but by hinting that his honour was compromised'. The two are linked since his imagined cuckoldry destroys his self-esteem, his standing in the eyes of other men and his position in society. Othello cannot bear the idea that he is keeping a part of the thing he loves for others' use, or that others are laughing at him behind his back. At the time a man's honour was inseparable from his wife's behaviour, and he was judged as much by how she was publicly perceived as by his own professional competence.

Top ten quotation

That it is his friend and subordinate, Cassio, who is implicated is a key factor in Othello's mental torture. This means that he thinks he is being betrayed on sexual, personal and professional levels, and therefore suffers a triple attack on his honour. Iago manages to persuade Othello to side with the '**cause**' of men against women, so that the final justification for the murder of Desdemona is the need to protect male honour generally: 'Yet she must die, else she'll betray more men' (5.2.6).

Because of the two possible meanings, 'honest, honest Iago' can be taken as a kind of pun. In the newer sense of the word meaning open and in touch with natural desires, he could be called honest in that he describes and acts out the crude urges of human nature. By comparison with Cassio, Othello and Roderigo, he could also be perceived as being manlier, another sense of honest, in that they put on airs and graces and use elaborate courtly and poetic language, while Iago's speech is blunt. He despises the foppish affectations of Cassio and the slavery of Othello to the 'captain's captain', Desdemona, and thinks that they dishonour the profession of the soldier.

Honest, when applied to women, meant chaste and faithful to one's husband, and Othello and Iago use it repeatedly in this sense. Desdemona is accused of double dishonesty, of lying and of laying with other men, as though one is a symptom of, and therefore evidence of, the other. As the *Penguin* introduction points out (Kenneth Muir (ed.), 1996 edition, page 24), this is a drama of marital, parental and professional honour, while the national honour of Venice is also at stake. It would therefore not be difficult to argue that the theme of honour and honesty is at least as important as jealousy in the play, and one that has wider applications and implications in the tragedy.

Appearance and reality

Though the characters in *Othello* construe everyone else's smiles, gestures and behaviour 'quite in the wrong' (4.1.104), the audience is given the responsibility of interpreting them correctly. Nearly every scene in the tragedy refers to or depends upon a character seeing and knowing something of someone. Many Elizabethans believed that external appearance revealed inner reality, but

Shakespeare was interested in exploring a fair exterior that concealed inner foulness. His plays explore the issues of good and evil and of truth and falsity, particularly in the major tragedies. *Othello* is asking how much one can ever know, how much one can bear to know, and how what we think we know can be distinguished from its opposite, which looks the same. René Descartes pointed out that we believe dreams to be true until we wake up, and as Ludwig Wittgenstein commented, the sun circling the earth would look the same as the earth circling the sun. Othello puts complete faith in the handkerchief as proof of Desdemona's infidelity. He says, 'I'll see before I doubt' (3.3.194), thinking this rational decision to test a hypothesis and to require 'ocular proof' will protect him from deception and reveal the truth. However, his dependence on the evidence of his eyes (for example, he took Desdemona's tears as proof that she pitied him) deprives him of his analytical faculties.

Iago is the arch-illusionist and has a magician's sleight of hand that deceives the eye. But Othello and Venice are also not what they seem, with an unpleasantness below the surface not acknowledged or known to be there. Like Iago, but for different reasons, Othello comes to consider 'mere suspicion' to be adequate evidence and becomes dependent for his supposed knowledge on his own senses and the deluding demon of Iago. Several characters have shock awakenings when the scales fall from their eyes and they see a loved one in a new and opposite light. Iago destabilises Othello's trust and faith by exposing them as irrational substitutes for knowledge and no match for apparent counter-evidence of a visible and tangible kind.

The Delphic Oracle exhorted the Ancient Greeks to 'know thyself' and this is a recurrent issue in classical tragedy as well as in Shakespeare's plays. A failure of self-knowledge extends to being unable to know anyone else, to judge oneself or others, or to question one's beliefs, which means a lack of the moral understanding that distinguishes humans from animals. Othello use the verb 'know' three times in his first speech; 'know' in its various grammatical forms is used 96 times in the tragedy. The paradox of not knowing yourself is that you do not know that you do not know, and can therefore do nothing to avoid becoming prey to others and to circumstance. Had he been aware of his propensity for sudden jealousy, Othello might have been less overcome by it. He seems ignorant of the fact that appearances can be ambiguous and deceptive, and neither forewarned or forearmed of the way Moors were perceived in Venetian society of the period. Othello cannot see himself except as the reflection in Desdemona's eyes, as a romantic hero, without flaws or weaknesses, or as a black visage, until the end.

W.H. Auden claimed that Iago is motivated by the desire to know and show what Othello is really like behind the mask of the celebrated warrior and joyful lover. By exposing the weak human hiding behind the façade of reputation he can both avenge himself on Othello and prove the hypocrisy of humanity, thus vindicating his sordid vision and justifying his own attitudes and behaviour as

Build critical skills

In the tragedy of *Othello*, self-knowledge is an important theme. Do you believe that any of the three major characters displays real self-knowledge? If they truly had self-knowledge, could tragedy be averted?

being honest by comparison. The amoral Iago knows that he has to demonstrate that noble abstract virtues do not exist, ethics are an affection and love is merely 'a lust of the blood', in order to maintain his self-esteem. Since these are things he cannot, for various reasons, have himself, he is driven (like Satan) to destroy the paradise from which he is excluded. The question is whether the Othello he reveals is the true Othello or a monster created by Iago, which did not previously exist.

Othello tries hard to justify himself after the tragic murder of Desdemona by saying 'Iago knows'. He thinks he means that Iago knows his wife and Cassio have committed adultery, but of course, Iago knows that they have not, which draws attention to the problem of meaning and usage of the verb 'to know'. In a wider sense he is implying that Iago is the 'knower' in the play, the repository of facts and wisdom, the counsellor and watcher who has power and authority because of his knowledge. Iago knows more than the other characters know themselves — how others feel about them, their present, future situations — and can predict their responses with what seems to be a supernatural prescience. He knows things that he cannot explicably know, such as the details of the elopement, Othello's imminent posting to Cyprus and Bianca's feelings for Cassio, but he does so by being alert and observant the whole time, by accurate character assessment and by his understanding of human nature. The tragedy is that nobody else knows this.

There is disagreement about just how much Emilia knows. For example, in Act 5, Scene 2 real surprise would look the same as fake surprise, so we cannot be sure whether she knew of Iago's plans for the handkerchief. In Cinthio's version of the story she does know, and Honigmann is inclined to think that Shakespeare's Emilia also knows (she calls her husband 'wayward' — 3.3.296), but is too frightened to speak out; Iago has ordered her to plead ignorance about the theft: 'Be not acknown on't' (3.3.322). That she is, however, deceived in her estimation of her husband is suggested by her appearing to believe that Iago is sorry about Cassio's dismissal, and it is unlikely that she would curse her husband, even in pretence (Act 4, Scene 2), since curses were taken very seriously and could not be undone. That she calls her husband nothing worse than 'wayward', meaning capricious, suggests that she does not fully understand his capacity for evil.

Limited vision

Honigmann entertains the possibility that Othello may be short-sighted. In Act 1, Scene 2 Iago tells Othello who is approaching twice (although in line 34 Othello recognises Cassio and the Duke's servants), but this may be Iago's way of getting in first with knowledge and making himself indispensable, rather than Shakespeare wanting to suggest that an active military commander is vision impaired through age. It prepares us, however, for the difficulty of establishing true identities in the play, especially in the dark, and for the realisation that Othello cannot see clearly in a metaphorical sense (this concept is used again in *King Lear*) when Othello asks Iago, 'Was not that Cassio who parted from my wife?' (3.3.37) it does not mean he is not sure who it was but that he is surprised, and this question also serves as a device to allow Iago to seize his opportunity to sow the seed of suspicion. Othello becomes dependent on Iago to be his literal and metaphorical eyes and reports sights to him, complete with an interpretation. As a result, Othello comes to see the world in the limited and negative way Iago sees it.

However, it could be claimed that, metaphorically, all the characters except Iago have impaired vision. Othello misjudges Iago, Cassio, Desdemona and Emilia. Desdemona miscalculates her father's reaction and loses him, as well as being unable to tell what is bothering Othello and attributing it to pressures of work, wrongly believing him incapable of jealousy; she does not suspect that her maid is untrustworthy and a liar, and does not realise that Iago is the last person she should turn to for help.

Metaphorically, all the characters, except Iago, have impaired vision.

The need to know

The Tree of Knowledge in the Garden of Eden tempted Adam and Eve, with Satan's help, to lose their innocence and bliss by eating the forbidden fruit. Likewise, Othello succumbs to the desire to know, finds doubt intolerable, and is therefore unable to resist the apple of knowledge the serpent Iago holds out to him. Othello cannot bear it that Iago 'Sees and knows more, much more than he unfolds' (3.3.246–7) as this makes Iago superior. Curiosity is a basic human drive and Iago destroys Othello by asking the simple question 'How do you know your wife is honest?' and implying that he knows differently.

Thinking and knowing, both ubiquitous words in the tragedy, are not the same, though Othello starts out believing that they are because of his trust in rationality. Iago's final torture of Othello is to refuse to give him the knowledge of why he did what he did; his final utterance is, ironically and tellingly, **'what you know, you know'**. One cannot both know and remain innocent, because knowledge involves acknowledging evil, hence the expression 'ignorance is bliss'. Othello would not have minded the whole camp enjoying Desdemona carnally, 'So I had nothing known' (3.3.351). Excessive knowledge corrupts, but a little knowledge is a dangerous thing and makes one desperate for more, and so vulnerable to manipulation by the 'knower', who can turn a tranquil mind into that of a 'credulous fool'.

> Top ten quotation

Nature erring from itself

One of the play's major paradoxes, as in the other main tragedies, is that nature itself is unnatural. Desdemona is the main representative of this in the play, being a 'fair devil' in three men's eyes, four counting Roderigo. According to her father and Iago – and, ironically, Othello, in the end – her love for Othello proves that she is unnatural. As Iago says, 'she would never have loved the Moor' if she had been 'blessed' because he is perceived by the Venetians as an abnormality, and natural taste would incline her towards the younger, whiter and more handsome Cassio.

The major paradox is that nature itself is unnatural.

Desdemona's unconventionality is also evidence of her unnaturalness. She goes against accepted codes of female behaviour in her society by being unfaithful to her father, forward with her suits and outspoken in the Senate. At that time, women were in tune with nature if they were maidens or mothers (that is, pure or fertile), but accused of being unnatural if they were spinsters, childless wives or whores (that is, ugly and rejected by men, barren or promiscuous). Othello is a product of nature, yet his skin colour renders him unnatural. Iago has inhuman qualities that cause him to be considered a devil, yet he too is man of woman born. All three of the main characters attract the word 'monstrous' (a word much used in the other major tragedies), meaning not just horrible but an aberration of nature, which highlights the paradox that a monster can only exist in and be created by nature, yet is to be feared.

All three of the main characters attract the word 'monstrous'.

The handkerchief

Thomas Rymer in his *A Short View of Tragedy* (1693) summed up *Othello* as 'so much ado, so much stress ... about an handkerchief' and asked, 'Why was this not called the tragedy of the handkerchief?' The handkerchief is, however, more than just a square of cloth; it means different things to different people and is an indicator of character, a test of relationships, the key to the plot and a symbol of major themes in the tragedy.

A handkerchief in those days was often an heirloom or part of a dowry, hand-made from expensive fabric, usually silk, and personally embroidered. Only the nobility possessed such a luxury item. Larger than today's handkerchiefs, it would not be used for blowing one's nose but as a decorative accessory. Its role in medieval literature was as a romantic love token either given to a suitor or dropped to provoke a chivalrous response.

Only the nobility possessed such a luxury item.

Desdemona's handkerchief was, according to Othello's romantic account, woven by a year-old sibyl (a female prophet) using silk from sacred worms and dye from the hearts of mummified virgins. However, he then tells two versions of the story: that his father gave it to his mother and warned her that if she lost it his love for her would die; that an Egyptian gave it to his mother and told her that it would subdue his father, and that she gave it to Othello on her death to pass on to his future wife. Othello is lying to Desdemona, consciously or unconsciously, as both versions cannot be true; he is also expressing his primitive beliefs for the first time. Being spotted with strawberries, the handkerchief could represent blood droplets on white sheets, a depiction of deflowering or the 'fruits of love' Othello is looking forward to on the wedding night, but that afterwards he may retain in his mind as an image of Desdemona's impurity.

For Othello the handkerchief is a romantic object he gave to Desdemona and asked her to cherish, therefore to him it is a symbol of his love for her and of the faith and trust that bind their marriage; by losing it she is rejecting him. It is also a sentimental link with his mother, a symbol of his parents' marriage, an 'antique token' linking him to his childhood past, a superstitious talisman of a magic that must be respected or something precious will be destroyed. The loss of the handkerchief equals not only the loss of love but the loss of Desdemona's soul ('perdition'), as he sees it. It is conclusive evidence of his wife's adultery. On the other hand, by rejecting it as 'too little' he rejects Desdemona's attempt to minister to him and therefore her love. He causes it to fall to the floor and lie unnoticed so that, ironically, he is the one who separates her from it and causes the chain of tragic events stemming from its loss.

For Desdemona it is a love gift, a lucky charm to make Othello love her as his father loved his mother, and her only link with his family and his past. It suggests her immaturity that she treats it as a child treats a comfort cloth and is unable to be parted from it.

Shakespeare makes Emilia pick up the dropped handkerchief rather than have Iago find it, which adds many extra dimensions to the play's relationships and coincidences. Because Emilia also hates Othello's and her mistress's 'most filthy bargain,' it is plausible for her to take the handkerchief to spite the original owner of it as an unconscious undoing of the marriage. Her part in the theft draws attention to her problematic relationship with Iago and her need to please her husband (a social reality despite her views on marriage).

▲ It is plausible for Emilia to take the handkerchief to spite the original owner. Amanda Harris as Emilia in the 2004 Royal Shakespeare Company production

Build critical skills

Try to imagine if there had been no handkerchief. Would Iago have been able to persuade Othello so swiftly of Desdemona's infidelity? How else might he have tried to achieve this? This might throw light on the importance of the handkerchief in the plot.

Target your thinking

- How does Shakespeare use characters to develop themes? (**AO1**)
- To what extent does contextual understanding shape your response to the characters? (**AO3**)
- In what ways have critics and actors (or directors) interpreted Shakespeare's characters? (**AO5**)

Othello, the Moor

Shakespeare constructs Othello as a Moor originating in Morocco via Spain. He has been a mercenary soldier since the age of seven, is probably now aged forty-two and after various campaigns is a now a renowned general in the employ of the Venetian state. He is the tragic hero of the play. For nine months he has been waiting in Venice for his next mission and has passed his time by visiting Senator Brabantio's house to entertain him, and subsequently his daughter Desdemona, who Othello has just secretly married. Although he appears on stage much less than Iago, and to some audiences he is much less interesting than the villain, Othello is intended to be the main character of the eponymous play because Iago does not undergo change during the tragedy, but Othello does, and to a great extent.

There is a tragic ambiguity about the way Othello is presented, personified by the two Othellos we see in the play, although he is a servant to white masters and has apparently more 'primitive' origins, he has a high rank, an aristocratic bearing and the civilised skills of rhetoric. It has been claimed that Othello and Iago are the two faces of man, the good and the evil in human nature, and, conversely, that they are the same man, both suffering from the same psychological and psychopathic disturbance tragically triggered by the monster jealousy. Another possibility – given that Shakespeare endeavours to make his characters as real as possible, and real people do not always behave predictably and logically – is that Othello is meant to be a mass of inconsistencies, and he falls back on his childhood self when threatened and under pressure, as people tend to do.

> There is a tragic ambiguity about the way Othello is presented, personified by the two Othellos we see in the play.

Tragic noble hero, flawed egotist, or both?

The question that has divided critics throughout the twentieth and early twenty-first centuries has been was Othello devised by Shakespeare to be a noble hero, deceived by a superhumanly cunning Iago, or is he a deeply flawed egoist, responsible for his own tragic downfall? Iago mocks him for being weak and a 'credulous fool' and when he says, 'He's that he is' (4.1.270) – meaning violent, irrational and unable to control his passions – he is suggesting that this is the Moor's essential, savage nature. Elsewhere, however, Iago lists his virtues.

In 1904, A.C. Bradley presented the case for Othello being a tragic noble hero, worthy of our sympathy who, without Iago's interference, would have led a blameless existence. In 1952, F.R. Leavis argued against this view, asserting that Othello is neither noble nor a hero, that Iago could hot have had an effect if the character weaknesses were not already there, and therefore Othello cannot be admirable. Because Bradley claims that the proof of Othello's nobility lies in his capacity for absolute trust, the debate focuses on whether Othello really trusts Desdemona, as he claims to when he has her sent for and swears, 'My life upon her faith!' (1.3.295). For it to evaporate so quickly suggests that he never really trusted her, or that like religious faith and love, trust, when put to the test, can go as suddenly as it comes, or that jealousy is stronger than trust and will always defeat it. A trust that can be destroyed in twenty minutes is obviously flawed in some way. By contrast Desdemona never loses hers. Whether noble hero or flawed egotist, his tragic flaw is to succumb to jealousy and lose that trust.

It is essential to Othello's self-esteem for him to believe himself to be noble and have others believe it too, as honour is inseparable from nobility. Shakespeare appears to say that he fulfils the criteria by being successful, respected by his subordinates and superiors, and entrusted with the safety of the Republic of Venice. He is poetic, sensitive to nature, dedicated to his job and his religion. His entry into the play is impressive and carries authority, as does his speech to the Senate, which was an accolade from the Duke. He is familiar with the concepts of duty and salvation, justice and love, and with their importance.

However, there is also evidence for the claim that Shakespeare presents Othello to be lacking in nobility. He displays an emotional volatility and exceptional sensuousness, which would not be consistent with the contemporary view of how a noble character would behave, and consideration for others is not a character trait even his greatest admirers could claim for him. There are elements of excess in his personality, and he could be accused of excessive love for Desdemona. Brabantio charges him with being a 'foul thief', and it is questionable how noble it is to marry without permission. This itself, may well be the start of Othello's tragic fall. Striking a woman, and in public, was an indisputably ignoble act at the time, killing Desdemona is a violation against chivalry as well as of Christian principles. When Othello says, 'Cuckold me!', 'False to me!', 'And with mine officer!' there is a strong indication of pride and arrogance.

In tragic terms, Othello could be accused of hubris (pride), of wanting to be god-like, in his insistence on knowing more than he should want to know or is capable of bearing. He is over-confident in his abilities and judgement, and in his belief that his passion and appetites are under control. He has the arrogance to

▲ Until the late twentieth century, British productions of *Othello* often starred white actors 'blacked up' – as Laurence Olivier here in this 1964 stage production. This is now considered politically incorrect and offensive

believe he can take on and out-talk Brabantio, the second most important man in Venice, and offend Venetian sensibilities with impunity. He is tempting fate when he says, 'My life upon her faith' about a woman he does not know very well, and to her father. In short, he could be said to be heading for the fall of the tragic hero, which in his case takes the ironic form of his turning Turk, the lowest and most despised creature he can imagine, and who he has spent his whole life fighting.

Context

According to the medieval Catholic Church, the following sins led one straight to hell: pride, envy, gluttony, lechery, avarice, wrath and sloth. The primary sin displayed in this play is pride.

Race, ethnicity and character

All the characters call Othello 'the Moor', even Desdemona sometimes, drawing attention to his race and ethnicity. Comments are made or implied about his sexual appetite and performance (which he feels obliged to deny to the Duke), when Iago makes these comments, he frames them in gross animal terms. Another accusation made against black people was that they were incapable of reason, because they were primitive and undisciplined, and they indulged in sensuality and unbridled emotion. The Othello offered by Shakespeare has a tendency to weep and roar, with exaggerated physical mannerisms, and there is an emphasis in the play on Othello's sense of smell and taste, which links him to bestial instincts and appetites.

Othello makes many references to elemental forces of nature, such as the sun and moon, which suggests a latent paganism underneath his Christianity. The stereotype also included the idea that non-whites were childishly unstable in mood and feelings: 'these Moors are changeable in their wills' (Iago, 1.3.347–8). Othello's language and behaviour reveal a bloodthirsty disposition and savouring of violence, and he could be said to revert to primitive beliefs and instincts and lose the veneer of civilisation when under pressure, as shown by the handkerchief story and his reaction to its loss. He does not seem comfortable in society or indoors.

Othello's appearance in the play is delayed until three hostile characters – Iago, Roderigo and Brabantio, a cross-section of Venetian society – have given their condemnatory views of him, which makes Othello a tragic victim from the start. There are specific verbal racist insults used in the play: 'thick lips' (Roderigo 1.1.65), 'old black ram' (1.1.87), 'the devil' (1.1.90), 'a barbary horse' (1.1.110), 'sooty bosom' (Brabantio, 1.2.70) and 'most filthy bargain' (Emilia, 5.2.153). Iago, as ever, is more subtle and his abuse takes the form of gratuitous mention of his colour ('black Othello' 2.3.29), constant references to him as 'the Moor', and

In 2015, a production of *Othello* was put on at the Royal Shakespeare Theatre, which cast a black actor as Iago for the first time. Hugh Quarshie played Othello and Lucian Msamati played Iago

Othello makes many references to elemental forces of nature.

lascivious comments on his sexuality. Othello's consciousness of his race and ethnicity maybe a factor in his character and behaviour, perhaps only pretending to be confident, he may suffer from being 'the outsider'.

Shakespeare discourages a one-side interpretation of Othello as a warning against mixed marriage or condemnation of the Moors. By making his main character an experienced commander and an accomplished warrior who is physically impressive, attractive to men and women, poetic, imaginative, a devout Christian, a powerful orator and implacable enemy of the 'Ottomites', Shakespeare opposes or offsets cultural misconceptions of race and ethnicity. Since Iago is the metaphorical Turk, monster and 'black' man, Shakespeare is inverting racist prejudice at the time that evil is indicated by skin colour alone.

Honest Iago

Iago is constructed as the tragic villain of the play. Presumably Venetian, he is married, childless and a veteran soldier. He is an 'ancient' meaning an ensign, a junior military officer whose traditional duty is to be the standard bearer, that is, to carry the flag into battle. Iago is a Spanish name – like Othello and Roderigo – and that of the most famous saint in Spain: Saint Iago, who was known as the 'Moor killer' for his slaughter of Spanish Moors. He has previously suspected his wife (Emilia) of having a sexual liaison with both Othello and Cassio. He has been disappointed in his expectation of promotion, and now resents Cassio, who he does not consider to merit the rank of lieutenant. He has a low opinion of women, and professes to hate the Moor. He exploits Roderigo, who pays him to advance his cause with Desdemona, and persuades him that Cassio is his rival.

Iago is Satanic in his energy, intelligence and daring contempt for goodness. He also has, unquietly in the play, a sense of humour, a device that always wins over audiences. We cannot help but admire his daring and quick-thinking, while knowing we should disapprove of his amorality. 'Lucky' is perhaps a more appropriate fixed epithet than 'honest', since Iago has the luck of the devil and chance always seem to be on his side. Timing favours Iago throughout the tragedy, as do outcomes: 'consequence do but approve my dream' (2.3.59). Other actions by the characters are more a matter of his being able to predict their responses through clever guesswork based on knowledge of how their minds work, but that nonetheless makes them fall neatly into his trap, such as Brabantio's rejection of his daughter, Cassio's liking for pretty things and Desdemona's overdoing the pleading for Cassio's reinstatement.

Iago states that he is twenty-eight years old (1.2.311–12), which students usually find surprising. It is shocking for one so young to be so cynical, as it seems he cannot have enough disillusionments to justify such a low view of humanity, or be experienced enough to think he understands all the ways of the world. It is also worrying that he can treat his young wife with such contempt, as though he got tired of her many years ago, or view his senior in age, Othello, as his inferior in a culture that respected age and the wisdom thought to accompany it.

TASK

How important is it that Othello is black? Would the tragedy have worked equally well if he had been a white outsider, from, for example, Spain?

Context

Tragedies often end with characters taking their own lives after realising the mistakes they have made. This 'insight' can only seem to come at the end of the tragedy when the chaos is irreversible.

CRITICAL VIEW

Lots of critics suggest that Othello is more of a tragic victim than a tragic hero. To what extent do you agree?

▲ Laurence Fishburne and Kenneth Branagh as Othello and Iago respectively, in a scene from the 1995 film version of *Othello*

Sources for Iago's spite

In 1818, the critic Samuel Taylor Coleridge puzzled over the reasons for Iago's spite calling this search 'the motive-hunting of a motiveless malignity'; and concluded that Iago is just evil. However, Iago appears to have reasons for hating all of the other main characters of the tragedy, so there is a question concerning his main target. According to Bradley, Iago has a 'keen sense of superiority', which is thwarted and wants satisfaction, and his guiding resentment is of 'Othello's eminence, Othello's goodness and his own dependence of Othello,' so he makes his superior his puppet. The racial hatred for Othello is paralleled by a political hatred for the 'Florentine' Cassio, and there is equally strong misogyny to account for his need to defeat Desdemona. In some ways, Cassio with 'a daily beauty in his life' (line 19), most threatens Iago's position and self-esteem, as he can be most directly compared to him and found wanting as a fellow soldier, peer and white man. By the end of the tragedy, his target has become anyone who stands in the way of his execution of his plan to destroy lives and get away with it.

Bradley says Iago has a general 'spite against goodness in men', so while any virtue exists he attempts to eliminate it. It is as if he is suffering from a disease or addiction, or controlled by an external force, and his appetite for sadistic enjoyment and power grows by what it feeds on. Other critics point to the bungled attempt on Cassio's life as the turning point for Iago's successes, but even Emilia's and Bianca's arrival at this scene are handled by Iago without suspicion falling upon himself, and Emilia fails to prevent the murder of Desdemona and therefore Othello's suicide. It is true that Cassio is not supposed to survive, that Emilia's death may not have been intended, and that Roderigo taking a long time to die is unfortunate for Iago. However, his refusal to speak at the end still leaves him in a position of control, something he seems to value more than anything else, and therefore he cannot categorically be said to have failed.

Some critics and directors have seen Iago as a victim of 'otherness'. His problem could take the form of feeling inferior in his home city-state because of the upper-class milieu he is moving in, and of his having been rejected as Othello's number two by preference for Cassio. All the other male characters in the tragedy outrank Iago, are of higher social status and have greater wealth of education.

Iago refuses to show repentance at the end of the tragedy. His last words are, **'Demand me nothing; What you know, you know:/From this time forth I will never speak word'** (5.2.301). He regrets nothing, so there is nothing to say. He recognises that there are no satisfactory explanations of mitigating circumstances for what he has done, nor words to put it into; or else he believes the characters did it to themselves, were asking for it, and therefore he has nothing to feel guilty about and they do not deserve an explanation. He does not accept their right to ask to judge and punish him. His defiant stance is consistent with his first words in the play, and shows that Iago has not changed at all. He despises emotion, self-pity, weakness and subordination, so refuses to affect any of them and conveys an inhuman self-command, which frightens the audience, as well as the remaining characters. It is a final act of torture to withhold the information about himself that might help them to understand what has happened to them.

Desdemona

The central tragic victim, Desdemona, still a teenager, is friendless and motherless. Shakespeare presents her as having led a sheltered life of domestic duty under the watchful eye of her father, Brabantio. She is bowled over by the tales Othello tells of his military exploits and journeys, and conceives a desire to travel and experience the wider world. Her ill-fated name means 'the unfortunate' in Greek.

Desdemona is a Christian martyr who is pure, chaste, devoted to her earthly and heavenly lord and master, and who has the virtues of faith, hope and chastity. She is associated with light, which is divine but vulnerable. She is young, possibly in her late teens, and the verbal chastisement, physical punishment and withdrawal of love she suffers, could be viewed as putting her in the position of an abused child. Her role is to be sacrificed on an altar to redeem mankind though her domestic duties are more mundane, and she can only listen to romantic tales by slipping away from the household chores.

Being motherless, she is a literary stereotype, which also reflects the social reality that huge numbers of women died in childbirth then (and until the late nineteenth century). She is forced to deceive her father in order to win her freedom, but she is naive in choosing Othello; exogamy, marrying outside of one's race and community, was not something to be done casually at that time. She is also naive about marriage, refusing to believe that unfaithful wives exist, and there is doubt about how well she really knows and understands her husband. Iago has a hatred of her, but despite this she does not help her own case with her naivety.

His refusal to speak at the end still leaves him in a position of control.

Top ten quotation

Context

When thinking about Desdemona's naivety we also need to be acutely aware of the position of women in society at this time. It was incredibly difficult to contradict the power and authority of male figures.

Emilia

Emilia is a Venetian designated to be a maid to Desdemona and to travel to Cyprus in the company of her husband, Iago. She desires to please Iago, despite his questionable treatment of her in private and in public. She becomes loyally attached to Desdemona, despite having stolen her handkerchief and having lied about it. Shakespeare constructs her as another tragic victim.

Emilia has the worldliness and resignation of her station as a servant and the desperation of the childless, unloved wife. She bitterly describes relationships between men and women as being best seen in terms of consumption: **'They are all but stomachs, and we all but food'**. She gets caught by the demands of her husband and is forced to lie, but finally chooses good over evil when it is too late. She conveys the gender inequalities within marriage and in conventional public behaviour, and represents the stereotype of the dismissed, silenced woman who finally fights back, but is killed by the patriarchal system for her temerity in doing so.

Top ten quotation

Build critical skills

Desdemona is usually presented as being older than a teenager in most contemporary productions. Othello is normally presented as being younger than forty-two. Why do you think this may be so?

Bianca

Bianca is part of the established Venetian community in Cyprus with her own lodgings. Cassio visits her there and falls in love with her. The dramatist has her unwittingly playing a role in the damning of Desdemona with the missing handkerchief as Cassio gives it to her to copy. As a courtesan (a high-class prostitute) who falls in love with her client, she reflects the paradox of Venetian sexual morality. As a sexual mercenary she could be said to ply a 'trade' for profit in the same way as the men of war do, yet it is seen as being indicative of her general moral character. She causes Cassio to reveal himself to be of dubious integrity in not wanting Othello to see him 'womaned', and it is ironic that she is disapproved of and accused of dishonesty by the less than honest Iago and Emilia. Bianca is part of the collateral damage of the tragedy. She is fortunate in not being killed.

Cassio

Michael Cassio is a Florentine, making him, like Othello, a mercenary and an outsider. Florentines were considered to be of higher social standing because of the city's cultural reputation. Shakespeare's key construction of him is as a theoretical and inexperienced soldier (Iago labels him 'a great arithmetician'), but chivalrous and educated: a gentleman by contrast to Othello and Iago. He becomes governor of Cyprus at the end and is made responsible for the torture of Iago. In some senses, Cassio is lucky to have survived the tragedy, considering Iago's plot against him.

TASK

Cassio plays a pivotal role in the plot of the tragedy. Without him, could Iago have turned Othello against Desdemona so swiftly? Do you find him a rounded and consistent character?

Roderigo

Roderigo is presented as a wealthy fool soon parted from him money, despised by Iago as 'poor trash of Venice', rejected by Brabantio as a suitor for his daughter. He thinks he is in love with Desdemona and resents the fact that she has chosen a black man over himself. At Iago's instigation he sells his land and follows her to Cyprus. Iago uses him to discredit and attack Cassio, and then kills him when injured. Only on his death does he understand that Iago has exploited him, and that Desdemona never received his jewels or messages. Shakespeare has him providing written evidence against Iago before he dies. Like Othello, Roderigo's tragic flaw is his naivety and belief in 'truth' despite what he is seeing on the ground. He is eventually caught in the crossfire of the tragedy.

Brabantio

Shakespeare constructs Brabantio as a leading senator of a group of ten councillors, under the leadership of the Duke of Venice, responsible for governing the Venetian empire. He enjoys control and has a high opinion of his own status and the city-state of Venice. He has strong views on who is an acceptable marriage partner for his only child, Desdemona, and would rather disown his own daughter than accept her marriage to a Moor. He dies of grief, either for his lost daughter or his lost reputation. Brabantio's death signifies that although he is not a major character in the play, tragic events also affect him. His tragic flaws are his absolute wish for control over his daughter and his own inherent racism towards Othello.

Minor characters

Montano was the governor of Cyprus, prior to Othello's arrival. Shakespeare gives him an important function in the plot, since he is treacherously manipulated by Iago to believe that Cassio is a drunkard. He tries to prevent Cassio from fighting with Roderigo and for this he is injured. Despite suffering minor effects from the wider tragedy, he eventually discovers Iago's treachery.

The Duke of Venice (who is not named by Shakespeare) is a figure of authority, who takes the decision to send Othello to Cyprus. He hears Brabantio's case against Othello and favours Othello.

Lodovico is a kinsman of Brabantio. Shakespeare has him act structurally as a messenger who brings a message to Cyprus. His function is to be bewildered by Othello's striking of Desdemona and the chain of murders and treachery taking place. He eventually takes command of the situation but his actions prove too late to alter the tragic events.

Gratiano is another kinsman of Brabantio, and he accompanies Lodovico to Cyprus. Shakespeare presents him as Desdemona's uncle and laments her death, as well as raging against Iago at the end of the play.

Clown (who is not named) tries to cheer up Cassio after his request for musicians has been rejected by Othello. He acts as a go-between, taking Cassio's request to Desdemona to plead for him and bringing Desdemona's reply. Shakespeare uses him as some comic relief with the tragedy.

▲ Only on his death does he understand that Iago has exploited him. Dominic West as Iago and Brodie Ross as Roderigo at the Crucible Theatre, Sheffield, 2011

35

Target your thinking

- How does Shakespeare create dramatic effects in the play? (**AO2**)
- What are the main language features that Shakespeare gives to each of the main characters? (**AO2**)
- In what ways is your response to *Othello* enhanced by an understanding of tragedy? (**AO3**)

Form

Shakespeare and contemporary theatre

In the early seventeenth century, when Shakespeare wrote his major tragedies (*Hamlet*, *Macbeth*, *King Lear* and *Othello*), drama had generally become more political, satirical, violent and tragic compared to the more lyric tastes and pastoral works of the other Elizabethans. There was a growing fashion for artificial masque and elaborate spectacle in plays and poetry, an emphasis on bloodthirsty revenge tragedies in urban settings. However, wit, irony and sophistication of ideas were still paramount in the plots, characterisation and language of the theatre. Play-going appealed to all sections of the population; the poor stood as 'groundlings' below the raised stage, while the wealthier sat in boxes or galleries. King James I was a keen theatregoer and supporter of Shakespeare's company, the King's Men, and had a personal interest in witchcraft, religion and the role of the monarch. Contemporary playwrights catered for these tastes in their choice of subject matter and creation of characters.

Tragedy

Tragedy originated in Dionysiac choral song in Greece of the fifth century BCE. In tragedy, which involves disaster and multiple deaths, some undeserved, the events seem directed by fate, which ironically overrules the intentions and desires of human victims, and creates a sense of waste, when exceptional people become fallen and their qualities are lost. The course that each tragic hero believes will lead to success in fact leads to destruction. Tragedies usually start with a serious problem early in the plot – related to death, war or a failure of judgement – which develops into a catastrophic situation requiring further deaths and noble sacrifices in order that the previous status quo, with new participants, is restored. Tragedy has long been regarded as the highest genre of drama as it has a philosophical seriousness and requires a playwright to produce work at the full stretch of his or her intellectual powers.

TASK

Investigate the conditions of what it was like to attend a play during Shakespeare's time. In what way were conditions very different to how audiences now respond to a Shakespeare text like *Othello*? Construct a table or PowerPoint presentation to show these core differences.

In tragedy the events seem directed by fate.

In Shakespearean tragedies the initial conflict is caused by a mistaken decision (usually the protagonist's) based on fear or desire, made through his own free will and against advice or his own better judgement. It starts off a disastrous, irreversible and seemingly inevitable chain of cause and effect events as the hero falls from high to low.

Whereas time is a healing agent in comedies, it works against the protagonists in tragedy as coincidence and urgency, aspects of malign fate. Act 3 is usually the climax of the conflict, and thereafter a sense of impending doom is created by the feeling that time is speeding up and out of control until the hero's – and the audience's – recognition of a painful truth about humanity and the universe. Because high tension cannot be sustained relentlessly for two hours in the theatre, there are quasi-comic scenes even in the most serious of Shakespeare's tragedies, which serve as ironic juxtapositions. After the multiple body count (often at least five deaths) and restoration of justice and order, a trusted high-ranking character makes the final chorus-like speech summing up the tragic events and looking forward to a brighter future.

There are striking similarities between Shakespearean tragedies, particularly the four major ones, written between 1601 and 1606, of which *Othello* was the second. The parallels lie partly in their plots, which are based on children and parents losing each other: siblings, friends or couples being divorced; murders by relatives; spying and lying. Nature is also particularly important in the major tragedies, as a main source of imagery and the embodiment of paradox, being the origin of both health and disease, good and evil. In Shakespearean tragedy, uncertainty is of the essence, and fundamental human experiences and beliefs are questioned with 'mighty opposites' being cross-examined but no verdicts given. Along with the tortured heroes, we have to ask ourselves: What constitutes humanity? What are we here for? How can we tell right from wrong? Who is in control? We are asked for our moral awareness but not our moral judgement, since no one is in a position to judge fellow humans or claim to understand the universe.

Shakespeare's tragic heroes

The tragic hero must be someone of eminent rank within his own society – a king, prince, or military leader, such as Othello – someone 'better than we are' (according to Aristotle). In classical terms they become guilty of 'hubris', an act of presumption as mere mortals, their over-reaching is punished by Nemesis, goddess of retribution, and the audience is expected to respond in feeling 'the pity of it'. The 'noble hero' makes what Aristotle called 'an error of judgement' (Greek: hamartia), which has traditionally been translated as 'fatal (in both senses of the word) flaw'. The mistake is traceable to a character fault, and this, in unfortunate conjunction with circumstance and coincidence, causes the tragic hero's fall 'from happiness to misery'. During this fall he will undergo ironic and sudden reversals, which bring him up against the 'realisation of the unthinkable' (Leech).

> ## Context
> Evil or irresponsible acts committed by individuals spread to involve families, court communities and the nation, representing the contemporary belief in the connection between the microcosm and the macrocosm.

We are asked for our moral awareness but not our moral judgement.

TASK

Write a list of the qualities that make up a noble hero. How many of these do you see in Othello?

CRITICAL VIEW

Newman (1987, p. 144) suggests that the tragedy of Othello is derived from a number of 'assumptions; made both by others about him and by Othello about himself'. How do you respond to this view?

The sense of waste and loss comes from the fact that the hero has superhuman qualities in other respects and could have gone on to achieve great things. Because free will is involved, an accident of birth or fate alone cannot be blamed, making the retribution more complex and a cause of concern to all humans.

Shakespeare's heroes die ambiguously; they either achieve a kind of dignity by showing courage in their final moments, even though possibly continuing to labour under a delusion, or passively cooperate with the workings of divine necessity. The classical view is that, 'The tragic hero makes a fuss' (Leech) about what has happened to him and the injustice of the world, and dies fighting back rather than accepting the unacceptable. The other, Christian view is that by recognising this error, taking responsibility for it, repenting of it and accepting punishment, redemption is possible for the hero. In either case, tragic heroes express the hope that they will survive in the memory of their friends and state, and that their true story will be told with its mitigating circumstances to reduce their culpability and to prove that death can be transcended by fond memory, historical record or legendary status.

Some models of tragedy

One of the things the audience should feel when watching a tragedy like *Othello* is that somehow the world is a worse place without the tragic hero being part of it. Tragedies offer a bleak vision of life since they concentrate on failure, conflict and disaster. In most dramas of this type, three aspects are emphasised: suffering, chaos and death. Suffering is what the characters must endure in a tragedy. The audience watches how the suffering is created and how the central characters deal with their suffering. Chaos (which we might also term as *disorder*) can be both personal and social. In some tragedies the central character breaks down; in others the whole of society disintegrates, while in several both the characters and the society fall apart and collapse. Chaos usually leads to death.

At the end of *Othello* the cast and the audience are left staring at the reality of death and its consequences. In this way, tragedies are very ambitious plays because they carry huge subject-matter and themes. You might even consider tragedy important as a literary form because we know that all life eventually ends in death. At one point in the play Othello actually uses the word chaos, though the tone offered is a loving one. Desdemona has just left the stage and he almost jokingly says:

Top ten quotation

> I do love thee, and when I love thee not
>
> Chaos is come again.
>
> (3.3. 92–3)

The language here is predictive of their fate, and these words have a grim irony later on in the drama. After being misled by Iago, Othello becomes a psychological wreck who is filled with rage, doubt and fear. His nobility then gives way to the chaos of desiring revenge on those who have hurt him. Tragedy strikes Othello from 'nowhere' and when he finds out about the affair, it is like a 'bad dream'. There are two major problems (or flaws) with Othello: his pride and his honour. Both of these things could contribute to him self-destructing because of his arrogance and his refusal to see evil in others.

Different views of tragedy

It is important to remember that the opinions of successive generations of readers about *Othello* are always influenced by the time period they were writing in and by the trends of literary scholarship. For example, someone writing about an inter-racial marriage in the eighteenth century would probably have a very different view to someone writing in the twenty-first century. Therefore you should read all criticism with a degree of scepticism, keep an open mind and constantly look back at the text itself. Sometimes certain readings find themselves falling out of favour with the world of literary studies because ideas have moved on or new interpretations come into vogue. However, this does not mean that those readings suddenly become irrelevant or unimportant to consider. One of the most important commentators on Shakespeare's tragedies was A.C. Bradley (1851–1935), who has already been mentioned in this book. Bradley took a very character-driven response to tragedy. This has since been heavily criticised, but nevertheless, in his famous book *Shakespearean Tragedy*, which was originally published in 1904, Bradley makes some helpful points about the play, which have implications for other tragedies as well:

> Of all Shakespeare's tragedies, I would answer, not even accepting King Lear, Othello *is the most painfully exciting and the most terrible. From the moment when the temptation of the hero begins, the reader's heart and mind are held in a vice, experiencing the extremes of pity and fear, sympathy and repulsion, sickening hope and dreadful expectation.*
>
> There is no subject more exciting than sexual jealousy rising to the pitch of passion; and there is hardly any spectacle at once so engrossing and so painful as that of a great nature suffering the torment of this passion, and driven by it to a crime which is also a hideous blunder.

> (A.C. Bradley (1965 [1904]) *Shakespearean Tragedy*, London: Macmillan, pp. 143–4)

Bradley was a reader operating at the beginning of the twentieth century. For a critic operating in the middle of that century, you could look at Helen Gardner (1908–86). Writing in 1963, Gardner has this to say about Othello:

There are two major problems (or flaws) with Othello: his pride and his honour. Both of these things could contribute to him self-destructing because of his arrogance and his refusal to see evil in others. Locate and list examples of where this pride and honour can be found.

Othello is like a hero of the ancient world in that he is not a man like us, but a man recognised as extraordinary. He seems born to do great deeds and live in legend. He has the obvious heroic qualities of courage and strength, and no actor can attempt the role who is not physically impressive. He has the heroic capacity for passion. But the thing that most sets him apart is his solitariness. He is a stranger, a man of alien race, without ties or nature or natural duties.

(Anne Ridler (ed.) (1970) *Shakespearean Criticism 1935–1970*, Oxford: Oxford University Press, pp. 352–3)

A modern recent interpretation of the play is offered by Karen Newman, who has spent considerable time exploring the connection between race and sexuality in critical responses to the play over time. One idea that Newman puts forward is that Desdemona appears to enjoy sex – something that was considered unacceptable for women in Shakespeare's day. Furthermore, she enjoys sex with an outsider. Therefore many prejudices and stereotypes are turned upside down by their marriage:

In Othello, the black Moor and the fair Desdemona are united in a marriage which all the other characters view as unthinkable. Shakespeare uses their assumption to generate the plot itself – Iago's ploy to string Roderigo along is his assurance that Desdemona could not, contrary to nature, long love a black man. Even his manipulation of Othello depends on the Moor's own prejudices against his blackness and belief that the fair Desdemona would prefer the white Cassio.

(Karen Newman '"And wash the Ethiop White": Femininity and the Monstrous in Othello' in J.E. Howard and M.F. O'Conner (eds.) (1987) *Shakespeare Reproduced: The Text in History*, London: Routledge, p. 144)

From this you can see that differences of opinion and contradiction are part of literary studies. For example, Bradley sees *Othello* as a drama of 'modern life' yet Gardner compares him to being 'like a hero of the ancient world'. Newman goes one stage further by being more open about the sexual aspects of the tragedy. Crucially, she also uses a phrase 'contrary to nature', which, as we know, has considerable importance in many tragedies. The readings here also give an indication of ways in which you can write about tragedy. You should also begin to note that tragedies can be viewed from lots of different perspectives: character, structure, problems, cultural, materialist, identity and gender. Sometimes we can consider criticism from history and at other times look at more modern interpretations. A range of other readers' opinions helps us to reach our own view of the tragedy.

The dramatic structure of tragedy

We now know that tragedies usually contain a hero, a villain and a victim. There are other structural elements we can consider though. Like most dramas, *Othello* has a recognisable five-part dramatic structure that is used over and over again in tragedies that you will read. Put simply, this is:

◥ introduction

◥ complication

◥ climax

◥ understanding

◥ resolution.

In *Othello*, these structural components of tragedy are very recognisable. Within the play there are perhaps two climaxes to the action. The first is the point where Othello smothers and kills Desdemona, mistakenly thinking that she has been unfaithful to him, the second is where Othello takes his own life. Both of these sequences are very dramatic and most of the audience would agree that this is where the actual moment of the tragedy occurs. One further complication to the structure of most tragedies is the moment where the tragic hero undergoes a process of review and self-evaluation, realising what their fault has been, and how they might have prevented events from happening. This process of understanding often happens after the climax and before the eventual resolution. The resolution signals the dawn of a new period of time in the imagined world of the play, where hopefully the same mistakes will not be made.

▲ The first tragic climax is the point where Othello smothers and kills Desdemona, mistakenly thinking that she has been unfaithful to him. Chiwetel Ejiofor as Othello and Kelly Reilly as Desdemona in the 2007 Donmar Theatre production

TASK

Consider the structure of the play with the above concepts in mind. Where do you see them beginning and ending? List your results and compare these with other people's interpretations.

From these
ideas, Aristotle
identifies six core
components that
should be in a
tragedy:
- plot
- character
- diction
- reasoning
- spectacle
- lyric poetry.

Aristotle and tragedy

One of the most important discussions of the theory or concept behind tragedy is to be found in *Poetics* by Aristotle (384–22 BCE). Aristotle attempts to define and understand how the genre of tragedy works. He begins to define tragedy by commenting that a tragic drama is the 'imitation of an action that is admirable, complete and possesses magnitude'. He also notes that tragedy is a form of drama that excites the emotions of 'pity and fear'. Its action should be 'single' and 'complete', presenting a reversal of 'fortune', involving persons 'who are held in great esteem', and it should be written in 'language made pleasurable' (all quotations from Malcolm Heath (ed. and tr.) (1996) *Aristotle: Poetics*, London: Penguin, pp. 10–13).

Aristotle further suggested that when writing a tragedy, dramatists should be 'effecting through pity and fear the catharsis of such emotions' (Heath 1996, p. 10). Catharsis (or purification) is the term Aristotle applies on the way Greek tragedies worked – they should purge or sweep away the pity and fear brought about by the tragic action being performed. It is an emotional release that purifies the mind and body. In this way, Aristotle argued, the audience would 'learn' how to behave and run their lives. If you have ever cried during a film or performance, then you will have undergone the cathartic power of that piece of drama. In this sense, the drama you were watching must have been very powerful.

Not all readers and observers of drama agree with the concept of *catharsis*. The German dramatist and poet Bertolt Brecht (1898–1956) offered a valid argument against Aristotle, which suggested that rather than have the audience be purged in this way, tragedies should make people think about how best to alter and change the world. Brecht considered this process of purification to be an outmoded one. In Brecht's way, tragedies would educate – although judging from some of the observations of Aristotle, he appeared to realise this effect as well; hence why it was considered an Athenian citizen's duty to attend the theatre.

Taking it further ▶

Brecht's theories on the impact of tragedy are quite different to those of Aristotle and indeed Shakespeare. Research more online about Brecht's understanding of theatre.

In *Othello*, the play is an imitation of an action that is serious. It involves the accusation that Othello's wife is unfaithful to him, and culminates in the death of Othello, his wife Desdemona and a number of other characters. The play has a certain magnitude; it is set in glamorous and exotic Venice and Cyprus (compared to dull and dreary London perhaps) and contains characters of high status. The play is complete. The play reaches a full resolution. No sequel is planned because the surviving characters must negotiate their way in the 'new world order' of a Venice without Othello. Othello is a Moor (one of the play's central issues is that of racism) but he is also a successful military general in the service of the state. Desdemona is the daughter of Brabantio, a Venetian senator – so is also of high status. Therefore they are persons renowned and of superior attainments. The murder of Desdemona does arouse fear and pity within us as an audience because we know that she is innocent, and that Othello is mistaken. Therefore *Othello* fits the concept of epic or classical tragedy.

Very often, according to Aristotle, the disastrous results are brought about by the tragic hero making a mistake. That mistake is most often based on a tragic flaw in that character. With Othello, it was to put absolute trust in Iago, who was actually spinning a web of deceit. Aristotle named this tragic flaw hubris, a kind of excessive pride that causes the hero to ignore divine or important warnings, or to break moral codes – for example, many characters warn Othello of his self-deception but he chooses to ignore them. The mistake that is made is termed hamartia (error).

In many tragedies the natural order is broken irreversibly. One final point here is that it is because the tragic hero's suffering is then greater than the actual offence that the audience feels pity. They realise that they could have behaved in exactly the same way, and therefore feel sorry for the character enduring the suffering.

One final concept that is important in the work of Aristotle was that he identified three unities. These are action, time and place. In theory, the unities of action, time and place should 'compact' the tragedy with events happening very quickly, on a tight time scale, in the same place. Therefore the catharsis that the audience should feel is very concentrated. If the unities were too separate the tragedy might not have the same effect. Shakespeare kept the principles of the unities, but he adapts them slightly to increase realism. By now you should begin to see how Aristotle's arguments relate to what you know about *Othello*.

Though often present on examination specifications, *Othello* is perhaps not as popular as the other four great tragedies. It is commonly deemed to be more domestic and less universal, it is shorter than the others, and seen as narrower in scope and lacking profundity in its commentary on humanity. Unusually, there is no subplot or parallel plot in *Othello*, which intensifies the claustrophobic atmosphere along with the relatively small number of characters.

Structure

The division of Shakespeare's play into acts and scenes is not included in the earliest texts: the quartos. In the First Folio of Shakespeare's works, published in 1623, seven years after his death, act and scene divisions for many of the plays were introduced by the editors. *Othello* is unique in that the quarto was divided into five acts. But that these divisions were not written down does not mean that they were not included in performance. All actors and audiences at this time expected a play to be presented in five acts. By convention, a new scene commenced when the stage was empty of actors, or when there was a substantial change of characters.

CRITICAL VIEW

Newman used the term 'contrary to nature' when she was writing about the marriage of Othello and Desdemona. What she means is that sometimes tragic events occur because the characters and situations that occur 'invert' or 'break' the natural order. What do you feel about them being termed 'contrary to nature'?

TASK

How do you think Shakespeare creates the claustrophobic atmosphere in *Othello*? What purpose does he have in structuring the tragedy in this manner?

Shakespeare undoubtedly wrote his plays with a sense of shaping them into five acts. Generally, Act 3 marks a key turning point in the plot, as it does in *Othello*, where Scene 3 shows Iago coming in ascendant over Othello. Thereafter the pace quickens, the pressure builds up and the crisis and climax are revealed as the plot races to its conclusion. In the tragedies the inevitable message of the second part of the play is that time brings defeat, disaster and death; by contrast, in the comedies, the message is that time brings healing, resolution and peace.

Although a relatively short play, *Othello* subjects the audience to intense and prolonged dramatic tension because of its tensely wound structure. There are no changes of perspective, sub or parallel plots, or fully memorable comic interludes with fools, porters or gravediggers and such like, as there are in the other tragedies. So the audience is particularly conscious of the chain of cause and effect driving the play.

Double time scheme

Othello is often referred to as having a double time scheme; this means that some events could only realistically take place in 'long time' that is, over a period or weeks or even months, whereas others are placed in the context of 'short time', happening within a few hours of each other with specific time references attached. Acts 2 to 5 cover only 33 hours and the whole play seems to be condensed into a matter of days.

The voyage to Cyprus from Venice by the main characters would have taken several weeks, depending on winds, and Cassio says that Iago and Desdemona have arrived a week earlier than expected. Gratiano and Lodovico also travel to Cyprus with a new commission for Othello, after receiving news that the Turkish fleet has been destroyed, both of which would have taken time. There are allusions that suggest that a significant period of time has passed, for example, Emilia saying that her husband has asked her 'a hundred times' to steal the handkerchief, or Bianca accusing Cassio having not visited her for eight days. On the other hand, there are specific time references, which indicate that only one full night and one full day are spent in Cyprus before the end of the play. The double time scheme gives the play the advantages of both long and short time; plausibility for psychology, and events as well as an alarming pace and sudden, shocking contrasts. 'We must obey the time', says Othello (1.3.297), making himself subservient to it, as he does to Iago.

Time runs too fast from the beginning of the play, interrupting hours of love with the urgency of war and not allowing anything to be completed. The pace of the play isolates the characters and deprives them of the opportunity to communicate. When the play opens, an event has occurred that is already too late to reverse – and may have been impetuous – and it seems as though the marriage has started a swift chain of cause and effect, which pulls everyone else into the tragedy. The audience is swept along by the chronological logic of events, but the pace makes us feel uncomfortable.

> **TASK**
>
> What are the successes and difficulties of having this double time scheme at work in the structure of the play?

Iago's soliloquies contribute to the feeling of speed by their content, structure and positioning. He can cover several hatreds, plans and comments on humanity's failings in a few lines seeming to be not only reacting to the quick succession of events, but also creating them. He is able to give the impression that time and speed are on his side (Iago congratulates himself that 'My boat sails freely both in wind and stream' – 2.3.60) that he is their agent or vice versa.

> Iago's soliloquies are the links and driving force of the plot.

Language

Doubles: language and meaning

Verse is language that is rhythmically organised according to particular patterns of metre and the arrangement of lines. Prose is discourse that is not constructed according to any measurable pattern and is not set out in lines but can still have a rhythm. In plays of Shakespeare's time and earlier, verse was the conventional medium of all literary discourse, including drama, and his plays all consist largely of blank (unrhymed) verse.

Rhyming couplets are used at the ends of scenes to give them an air of finality – often sinister – or for spells, songs or some other special form of discourse. Couplets also suggest common wisdom is being quoted, as in Act 1, Scene 3 when Brabantio and the Duke of Venice exchange sententious advice. Prose was generally reserved for characters of lower social status, for comic or domestic scenes, or to indicate secrecy or conspiracy (Iago and drunken Cassio communicate in prose, and Iago and Roderigo when plotting in Act 2, Scene 1).

The monotony of several hours of blank verse is avoided by metrical irregularities, incomplete and shared lines, enjambment, caesuras and stress reversals; these all obscure the normal verse rhythm and give variety, so that the audience is usually not conscious of the play's dialogue being mainly in verse. Close analysis of the verse reveals that these techniques, as well as having a dramatic effect, can indicate the characters' attitudes and feelings. It is always significant and needs to be interpreted if a character who normally uses verse switches to prose and vice versa. Characters who suddenly become less fluent, articulate or capable of speaking in a smooth rhythm are often undergoing emotional disturbance or rapid thinking. This is particularly noticeable in Othello's speech in Acts 3 and 4, and in Iago's incomplete line (5.2.180). You should be aware of the prose sequences in the play and the effect caused by their contrast with what precedes and follows in each case. You also need to note which characters rarely use or are uncomfortable with prose, such as Desdemona, and which change according to their interlocutor or context, such as Emilia. Iago moves easily between verse and prose, as one would expect.

There are different types of prose in terms of register and complexity of syntax and this plays a role in the definition of character. A formal register used in an intimate situation, such as Othello to the sleeping Desdemona at the beginning of Act 5, Scene 2, is often an indication that the character wishes to distance

Context

In Shakespeare's plays verse tended to be given to noble and royal characters, to express romantic or elevated feelings, and at certain heightened moments they use rhyming couplets.

TASK

Examine the rhythms of the language in the play. Choose one soliloquy and then walk as you read it aloud. Stop walking when you hit a full stop, turn to the left when you hit a comma and turn to the right if you encounter any other piece of punctuation. Also try reading the soliloquies at different speeds and put emphasis on certain words. What effect does this have?

themselves from what they are doing and justify it. Colloquial diction in an official setting is equally odd and in need of comment, as in Act 4, Scene 1 when Othello talks inappropriately to Lodovico. Simple monosyllables, when repeated, convey intense and articulate feeling, such as Othello's 'O blood, blood, blood!' (3.3.454). When he uses the affectionate words 'wretch', 'wench' and 'my girl' of Desdemona the audience's attention is drawn to the chilling incongruity between language and action, highlighting the mental struggle.

Taking it further ▶▶

You might try translating one of Othello's or Iago's soliloquies into contemporary English. Use the glossary and notes in your edition to help you do this. What is lost and what is gained in the new version?

Iago has the ability to use language and events to kill two birds with one stone. In Act 2, Scene 3 he both condemns and excuses Cassio's fault, and in Act 3, Scene 3 he wins Othello's trust by offering support and sympathy, but he is actually insulting and belittling him. He simultaneously slanders Cassio and criticises Othello's lack of judgement to Montano in Act 2, Scene 3 while still giving the impression of being an honest and loyal friend to both. Setting up Roderigo to attack Othello could deliver double benefit to Iago if they kill each other. Getting Othello to kill Desdemona and then himself scores double points.

In a play dealing with duplicity, seeming and opposites, one would expect the language of *Othello* to contain elements of doubleness, the word 'double' is itself used several times, for example, 'double-damned' (4.2.37). Othello is sometimes called 'the General' and sometimes called 'the Moor', which draws attention to contrasting aspects of his character and the contradictory attitudes of others towards him. As well as two Othellos, there are two Iagos, the 'honest' Iago and the behind-the-scenes dishonest one. Iago likes puns and alliteration, and dabbles in doubling: 'parley to provocation', 'potations pottle-deep' and 'potent in potting' all occur in one scene (Act 2, Scene 3).

Top ten quotation ▷

Oxymoronic phrases show that paradox is built into the language of the play: **'Divinity of hell!'** (2.3.340), **'excellent wretch'** (3.3.90), 'fair devil' (3.3.481), 'this sorrow's heavenly' (5.2.21), 'an honourable murderer' (5.2.291) and 'honest Iago' (1.3.294). There are also several words in frequent use in the play that are ambiguous: lying (physically and verbally), committed (action and adultery), satisfied (logically and sexually), solicit (request and sexually importune), conceive (mentally and physically), credit (worth and belief), faithful (having faith and being chaste) and incontinent (immediate and unable to restrain sexual appetite). Iago is deliberate in his use of sexual innuendo and double entendre, as with 'soliciting' at the end of Act 2, but presumably Cassio and Desdemona are not; Cassio asks that Emilia will 'procure' him some 'access' to Desdemona (3.1.35–6).

Everything is double-sided.

Another group of words seem to dominate the play because of constant reiteration: there are 52 'honests', 29 'lieutenants', 25 'lies' and 'devils', and over 20 'beds'. Saying something many times gives it credibility, especially to the unsuspecting hearer or it suggests an obsession. To the suspicious it is conclusive evidence, and Desdemona's use of Cassio's name has this effect on Othello. Reiteration also contributes to the theme of excess, and parallels the duplication of events that include a double climax, for example, Iago's suspicion of Emilia's adultery; Desdemona 'hath deceived her father, and may thee' (1.3.291); Cassio being attacked by Roderigo; Desdemona being cast off; ships arriving from Venice; Othello killing the Turk. If something has happened once, it can happen again, logically, and this sets up a self-fulfilling expectation that it will.

Imagery

Shakespeare 's imagery repays close study, as each play has its own recurring group of images, in addition to the typical and traditional images of the Elizabethan and Jacobean periods, pertaining to heaven and hell, fire and water, and bonds and divisions. The language of the tragedies is dominated by life-threatening images of evil, poison, diseases and violence, which echo Biblical imagery. In Shakespeare's plays, images are often literalised metaphors, for example, Othello's blackness is both his actual skin colour and a representation of evil, and the conceptual adulterous bed becomes the real marital bed in the final act. In addition to reinforcing themes, imagery gives atmosphere and progression to the text, helps to delineate character, and provides integrity, pattern and meaning. The images in *Othello* tend to work in pairs of opposites, for example, dark and light, which can then be seen to reverse themselves or become indistinguishable from each other. Some key imagery in the play includes:

- animals
- black and white
- blood
- eyes
- gardening
- hell
- jewels
- poison
- pregnancy
- sea
- traps
- turning
- words.

TASK
Choose two or three types of imagery from the list and see if you can find examples of them within the text.

The different language of Othello

Roderigo describes Othello very early on as an 'extravagant and wheeling stranger' (1.1.134), meaning that he was perceived by the Venetians as exotic and extreme in his language as well as his appearance. His speeches to the Senate in Act 1, Scene 3 are grandiose public speaking, full of metaphor, hyperbole and the traditional archaisms and euphemisms of military diction, such as, 'steed'. His imagery is sensuous, cosmic and elemental relating to movement and size, it carries him and his listeners away. He commonly uses the first person pronoun and is egocentric in his relating of events and feelings.

▲ Iago speaks to the audience throughout the play, unlike Othello, and this draws us into his web. Rory Kinnear as Iago at the Olivier Theatre, Royal National Theatre, London, 2013

Nothing is certain or absolute.

TASK

Use one of Iago's soliloquies from the text and role-play him at this point in the play. Examine the different ways in which you might interpret the language here. Use varying speeds, tones and emphasis. What do you consider the best approach?

Later in the play his utterances become very different. Here is a selection from Act 5, Scene 2: 'Ha!', 'O misery!', 'Not a jot, not a jot', 'Ha, ha, false to me!', 'Death and damnation! O!', 'O monstrous! Monstrous!', 'I'll tear her all to pieces!', 'O, blood, blood, blood!', 'The handkerchief!', 'Zounds!', 'What? What?', 'O, I see that nose of yours, but not that dog I shall throw it to!', 'but yet the pity of it, Iago! O, Iago. The pity of it, Iago!', 'I will chop her into messes!', 'Fire and brimstone!' and 'I am glad to see you mad.'

In the second half of Act 3 (from 3.3.156) until he leaves in Act 4, Scene 2, Othello's speech reflects his wrath, mental pain and dependency on Iago, whose diction he is copying. Humans are reduced to 'Goats and monkeys!' The epileptic fit speech (4.1.34–44) and the one after he strikes Desdemona (4.1. 253–68) contain examples of most of the features of his growing inarticulacy: very short responses, simple or non-sentences, non-words, repetition, monosyllables, grammatical breakdown, contradictions, exclamation and cursing. This blasphemous language echoes Iago's first words in the play: 'S'blood'. Now he sees himself from the outside, through Iago's eyes, imagining that Desdemona shares this view, and his shaken confidence is indicated in his fractured utterance and the loss of his former fluency and rhetoric.

Iago's language

Soliloquies

The dramatic device of the soliloquy gives us the speaker's perspective and makes us in part, his accomplices, as we are taken into his confidence and listen to his plots being hatched against the other characters. Iago speaks to the audience throughout the play, unlike Othello, and this draws us into his web. The theatrical convention is that in soliloquy the characters tell the truth, but Iago may be an exception in that he may not know himself what the truth is about his own feelings.

Iago's soliloquies are an essential part of the plot of the tragedy in that they tend to fall at the beginning or end of scenes, where they either preview what is about to happen, or summarise and look back on what has just happened, and the response of the others. The strategic placing of the speeches gives the impression that Iago is playing the role of chorus in a play of his own devising, and that he is the source of all the action. His soliloquies repay close attention for the wealth of material they provide for a discussion of the characters, themes and imagery of the play, as well as for what they reveal about the audacity of his own mind.

The art of persuasion

In Act 3, Scene 3 Othello is persuaded within 150 lines not only to doubt his wife's fidelity, but also to have her spied upon; within another 250 lines he has bonded himself to Iago, and a few minutes later he has sworn to murder

Desdemona that same evening. The number and range of persuasive devices employed by Iago, both in choice of words and types of strategy, combined with the overactive imagination and insecurities of Othello, make this less surprising than many critics have claimed. Iago appeals to Othello's logic and rationality, while actually manipulating him psychologically and emotionally, until he creates a dependency in Othello. Othello believes that Iago is sympathetic to his cause, and when Iago swears to do anything Othello asks of him to show his support, Othello allows Iago to replace Desdemona in his esteem and affection, as his confidant and soulmate.

The skills and advantages that enable Iago to be so successful in what critics call the 'temptation' scene are the satanic powers of both linguistic and psychological manipulation. The sheer weight of words also needs to be taken into account, since Iago has 90 lines to Othello's 60, giving him the upper hand in the dialogue in which the content and reactions are determined by Iago and have been planned by him in advance. Iago has fluency of expression and of ideas, a slickness of tongue and mind, and a skill in insinuation such that what is implied cannot be disproved nor held to his account. As an actor he also has confidence in delivery, the ability to put on a mask and the gift of improvisation to enable him to take advantage of any opportunity. In addition, Iago is a soldier who knows from experience when to feign a retreat in order to advance further.

Iago's tactics and intentions are collectively to imply some hidden unpleasantness, to put a different complexion on something to make it seem less innocent, or to present a hypothesis as if it were fact. He builds up a case against Desdemona and Cassio from purely circumstantial evidence. He is most fittingly described as *advocatus diaboli*, the devil's advocate. He chooses phrases judiciously to have maximum visual effect in Othello's mind and yet simultaneously to appear to be concrete, objective and 'probal to thinking' (2.3.332) such as the repeated use of 'other proofs', which do not actually exist. He creates unbearable tension and suspense through delaying giving answers, which not only makes Othello more desperate for information ('Would I were satisfied!' – 3.3.394), but more likely to believe it when he does get it.

Iago's persuasive devices lead his 'ass' Othello through a sequence of emotional stages in the 'temptation scene', starting at 3.3.90 when Desdemona leaves a love-struck Othello, who is apprehensive about what would happen if he should lose her. Iago's most repeated words in Act 3 are 'kiss', 'honesty', 'bed', 'foolish' and 'man'. These turn abstract love into physical sex, which by extension and implication inevitably lead a fool who thought his wife was honest to the realisation and visualisation of his wife in bed with and being kissed by another man.

Target your thinking

- In what ways can analysing *Othello* within a broad range of contexts deepen your textual understanding? (**AO3**)
- How can your understanding of contexts enable you to explore different interpretations of the text? (**AO5**)

Biographical context

William Shakespeare was born in 1564 in the English town of Stratford-upon-Avon. He was born to relatively well-off middle-class parents and was educated at the local grammar school, where among other subjects he learned Latin. He was born early in the reign of Queen Elizabeth I, whose reign epitomised a Golden Age in English literature and culture. The Renaissance in the Arts had started in Italy more than a century earlier and Shakespeare's works are imbued with the spirit of his age.

After leaving school, Shakespeare married Anne Hathaway before moving to London, the heart of a rapidly growing theatrical world, and becoming an actor. He started writing plays of his own shortly after. Very little is known with certainty about his life, but he became quite a wealthy man and owned a fine house in Stratford. He died in 1616, succeeded by two daughters; his only son Hamnet, died as a child.

He wrote 37 plays in all, as well as a number of poems, which includes a celebrated sequence of sonnets. He remained an active member of the King's Men theatrical company until shortly before his death.

Historical context

Shakespeare wrote many of his early plays during the latter years of Elizabeth's reign. On her death in 1603, she was succeeded by James I, the former king of Scotland, and many of Shakespeare's most celebrated plays, including *Othello*, were written during the years immediately before and after the change of monarch. When thinking about the tragedy of *Othello* it is always good to consider this 'moment of production' and relate the play to its religious, social, political, economic and historical context.

The Venetian Republic and the Turkish threat

While the remainder of Europe was ruled by monarchs and feudal lords, the northern part of Italy was unique in being organised into 'city-states'. Venice was one of the most celebrated of these; the first Doge (Duke) of Venice was elected in 727 and the Republic of Venice survived for more than 1,000 years. The republican Venetians elected a Grand council composed of the most prominent citizens, which in turn elected the Doge. Shortly before the year 1000CE, Venice began to exploit its position at the head of the Adriatic Sea to found a seaboard empire that would eventually stretch to Levant (the eastern Mediterranean) and the shores of the Black Sea. The Venetian Republic fell into decline from 1570 onwards after the loss of Cyprus to the Turks. The position of Cyprus at the crossroads of the eastern Mediterranean helps to explain its history of invasion and subjugation over a period of 4,000 years.

The Christian world – Europe, North Africa, Levant and Asia Minor – began to be threatened by Islam almost immediately after its creation in the seventh century, Muslims rapidly conquered all the non-European areas, struck deep into Europe before they were defeated in France. The Christians launched a campaign to win back the holy places of Jerusalem from the Muslims in 1097 and achieved temporary successes. It was these crusades that first brought Europeans to Cyprus, which they colonised as an ideal base for operations in the Levant. The Ottoman Turks mounted increasingly powerful operations against the Christians from the fifteenth century, and in 1453 symbolically conquered Constantinople, the capital of the Byzantine Empire. The remainder of Greece and most of the Balkans fell soon after, leaving Cyprus as a dangerously isolated Christian outpost in the Muslim world. The Turkish invasion of the island in 1570–1, when Othello is set, consolidated Ottoman control of the region and they henceforth dominated the eastern Mediterranean. The implications of this conflict are still felt today.

Cyprus was a dangerously isolated Christian outpost.

Moors and Muslims

'Moor' and 'blackamoor' (a contraction of 'black as a Moor') were used very loosely in Elizabethan England to indicate any person of dark or black skin, including all people of African descent, but correctly referred to Muslims who originated from Morocco and who had conquered and settled in Spain in the seventh century CE. Parts of Spain remained Muslim and many Moors from North Africa settled there until the 'Moorish kingdom' of Granada was finally defeated by the Spanish kings in 1492, following which all remaining Moors were forcibly converted to Christianity as 'Moriscos'. With his Spanish name and the 'sword of Spain', it seems probable that Othello was a Morisco expelled from Spain and hence a converted Christian.

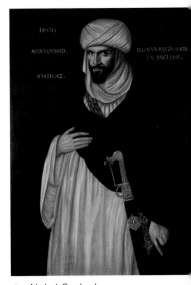

▲ Abd el-Ouahed ben Messaoud was the Moroccan (Berber) ambassador to the court of Queen Elizabeth I in 1600. He may have been the inspiration for the character of Othello

CRITICAL VIEW

Anne Barton (1993, pp. 214–16) observes that by the end of Othello, 'issues of the state are non-existent' and that the Turkish threat that dominated the early half of the play has disappeared. What is your view on this? Do you consider this realistic?

Build critical skills

Research the attitudes of mainstream English society in the Renaissance to individuals with different ethnicity or racial heritage.

There were two distinct ethnic groups involved in the Muslim conquest of Spain, and who hence came to be known as 'Moors'. The Berbers were the original inhabitants of the 'Barbary coast', the Mediterranean shore of north-west Africa (the word 'Barbary' is used three times in the play). They typically have much darker skins than Arabs or Berbers, although not as dark as central and southern Africans. Moors and Moriscos could be either Arabs or Berbers, and although it is uncertain what kind of Moor Shakespeare had in mind, the repeated references to blackness would hardly describe a stereotypical Arab. In August 1600, the ambassador of the King of Barbary and his retinue visited London and caused a stir with their appearances in public over the next six months. A contemporary audience would have been familiar with Berbers, and it is therefore likely that Othello is being depicted by Shakespeare as being a dark-skinned Berber. Negroes and blackamoors were considered a problem in England in 1601, when it was decreed that too many had 'crept into the realm' and had become an 'annoyance'. Elizabeth I ordered two edicts of deportation for their return to Barbary.

At this time black people were either represented as savages and monsters, only fit to be slaves, or as mysterious and exotic chieftains. Whether menacing or repulsive heathens or romantic and heroic warriors, they were considered dangerous and unnatural because they were foreign. Thomas Rymer's interpretation of the play in the late seventeenth century as a condemnation of women who run away with blackamoors shows how a black general being permitted to elope with an upper-class white woman 'upset all contemporary notions of decorum' and possibly indicates why the tragedy occurs.

Locations for tragedy: Venice and Cyprus

Act 1 is set in Venice but the subsequent four acts take place in Cyprus. The two locations in the tragedy are mentioned several times, and they are not only an integral part of the plot, but they are intrinsic to its characterisation and themes. As Shakespeare and his audiences would have known, Cyprus was definitely taken by the Turks a few months after the setting of the play in 1570, which adds the extra irony that the Venetian Republic has only temporarily averted the barbarian threat.

In 1600, Venice was approximately the same size as London and had many foreign residents and visitors because of trade links with the east and with North Africa. It was not only powerful and respected in eastern and western nations, but a byword for beauty, culture and civilisation. However, it was also thought of as pleasure capital and known for its sexual tolerance and courtesans.

The Senate, however dignified, is engaged in a war for profit and territory, and Othello and Cassio are mercenaries, killing for hire. There is other evidence of corruption caused by imperial ambition, wealth and complacency in Brabantio's

TASK

Examine the geography of the tragedy. What are the connections between North Africa, Spain, Venice and Cyprus?

imprisonment of his daughter for the purpose of arranging a good marriage, and Roderigo's 'unlawful solicitation' of Desdemona through the use of his money as bribes. Iago has also made money his replacement for morality, having hired 'three great ones of the city' to plead his suit for the lieutenancy – a position obviously not expected to be awarded on merit – and being a confidence trickster and pimp for financial gain. Venice is therefore a less virtuous place than it might appear, which sets the keynote for the play, and the 'super-subtle' Venetians do not invite much respect, all being obsessed with money and trading in human flesh, including Emilia, who thinks that adultery cannot be condoned if the price is right, and the ironically named Bianca (meaning 'white'), who sells her body for nice clothes. The corruption is a precept for tragic events.

In addition, the racism in the play is expressed by four Venetian characters: Roderigo, Iago, Brabantio and Emilia. When faced with something they cannot understand rationally, because it is 'unnatural', a leading Venetian senator falls back on the accusation of witchcraft, the veneer of civilisation is thin, and prejudice and superstition lurk just beneath the surface. This contributes to the play's theme of appearance versus reality, and to the idea that underneath the visible white surface lies blackness. It may be significant that the only winner in the play is Cassio, who is specifically distinguished from the others as a Florentine.

The location, history and atmosphere of Cyprus, where the tragic events occur, are significant to the themes of the play. Described twice in Act 2 as 'this war-like isle', Cyprus is apparently the antithesis to peaceful Venice. Less well-fortified than Rhodes, it is more vulnerable to the traditional Venetian enemy: the Muslim threat. Having always been a colony, Cyprus has never had autonomy and is therefore a symbol of submission. Since it was thought to be the birthplace of Aphrodite, goddess of love, it is an island of love dominated by war. As the last European bastion against the marauding infidels, it is isolated, occupied, under threat, and in a state of turbulence, with its people dependent and frightened. This is the mentality Othello falls into after his arrival there, thanks to the machinations of the 'Turk' Iago, who invades, captures and then subjects him to his rule. As the battlefield between the forces of Christianity and heathenism, Cyprus represents actual war and also the figurative thematic battles between good and evil, light and darkness, heaven and hell. It hosts two street fights, drunkenness, prostitution, murder, verbal and physical attacks on women, and a general loss of normality and decorum indicative of chaos, as if the transition from Venice to Cyprus has unlocked the primitive side of previously restrained characters, including Othello. Not one of the major characters returns from Cyprus to Venice within the play, as if it is not a journey that can be made in reverse, like the loss of virginity, trust and innocence. Cyprus is where European meets Turk, and loses the battle of civilisation and humanity.

CRITICAL VIEW

A.C. Bradley felt that the power of *Othello* for audiences of Shakespeare's day was that the play was, in fact, very contemporary. Unlike other tragedies, it was not set in the distant past. The date of the Turkish attack on Cyprus was in 1570, so within living memory of some watching it. What do you think the effect of this might be?

Social context

The role of women

Women's parts in plays did not equal men's in number, size or status because they were written for boy actors with unbroken voices, since it was unthinkable for women to perform on the stage. However, Shakespeare was interested in female perspectives and psychology, and women have significant roles in all the major tragedies as wives and daughters. None of them, however, live at the end of their respective plays.

Ownership

A woman's place was in the home and she had no role to play in the public arena. Women were possessions and were dependent on their fathers until they were handed over to the rule of their husbands, who they also had to love, honour and obey. Since women were considered to be naturally inferior in intellect and morality, their feelings or points of view were not considered; all decisions were taken for them and they were expected to accept them without argument and carry out the wishes of men. They had no or little education; Othello describes how their job was to be 'delicate with a needle' and 'sing the savageness out of a bear'. The consequences of not performing these daughterly and wifely duties were serious, involving being disowned and deprived of a home, financial support and a place in society; prostitution was often the only way to survive without a dowry or a supportive male relative. Women could only rise through their association with men and their rank; hence Emilia's assertion that she would commit adultery if it meant making Iago a monarch.

For women, male ownership meant being subject to restriction of movement and lack of control over their bodies. It was a man's worst nightmare to have a wife or daughter who caused the loss of his honour and status in the community through attracting gossip and besmirching her reputation.

Though they seem to represent three social levels, the women in the tragedy all accept that they are powerless and subject to male decree and patronage: Emilia has no choice but to accompany the party to Cyprus, as Othello has ordered it, and Desdemona could not have stayed in Venice, having been cast off by her father. Desdemona wants a different life from the one she was born to and that her father had in mind for her, but she has no more real control over her life than Bianca, who accepts her fate with the line, 'I must be circumstanced' (3.4.202).

Double standards

Social attitudes to male and female behaviour then, as now, were very different: male promiscuity, adultery, pre- or extra-marital sex were not condemned and considered natural. Cassio's consorting with a prostitute, whether married or not, would be commonplace, and not only expected of men generally – soldiers in particular – but even admired. Roderigo's death as a punishment for his foolishness, not for his 'unlawful solicitation' of a married woman, was licensed by medieval romantic literature. By contrast, fornicating women were considered a threat to the Church and to the fabric of society; they were blamed for leading men astray, destroying men's honour and bringing shame on the extended family. Women were thought to be easily seduced, being descended from Eve, the betrayer of mankind.

Critics have commented on the dislocation of love and sex the men in the play share, but that does not affect the women. Men wished to marry virgins and to have chaste wives for social reasons, but have whores available for their pleasure, thereby creating the dichotomy of two types of women, reputable and not. Women's social position was determined by their relationship to men and consequent sexual status. There were only four categories (with no equivalent male variations): maiden, wife, widow and whore. A fifth category – witch – was reserved for those not regarded as real women because of their masculine characteristics, ugliness or barrenness (see *Macbeth*).

Reputation, reputation, reputation

What distinguishes a respectable married woman like Emilia from a 'strumpet' like Bianca is not her appearance or social background, or even her sexual behaviour, but her reputation, that is, the label she is given by society. This made reputation an essential commodity for social survival, yet it was vulnerable to attack by any dissatisfied male. There was no forum in which calumny (defamation) could be contested and a reputation once lost could not be regained. The fallen woman became the prey of gossips, and was ostracised and excluded from polite society, necessitating suicide or entrance into a nunnery.

Silent victims

The virgin, newly-wed or demure widow was a target for predatory rakes and lechers whose conquest of the apparently unattainable was an irresistible challenge to their masculinity, and brides and betrothed women, being in a state of transition, were particularly vulnerable to assault and slander. Though the men were rarely punished, in reality or fiction, the conquered literary female had to die or be killed. Desdemona seems to be doomed at birth by her name, meaning 'unfortunate'. It is interesting that characters and audiences alike are concerned at the injustice of Desdemona's death on the grounds that she was not guilty, not because it would be unacceptable for her to be murdered, even if she had slept with Cassio. This silence renders women tragic victims.

Women were expected to be seen, but not heard, even especially in their husbands' or fathers' presence. Together, Emilia, with 245 lines, and Desdemona, with 388, have only half as many as Iago in the play. Between them, the women show the subordinate and passive position of women in Venetian society who must wait to be visited, proposed to, and sent for. Though they may have temper tantrums (Bianca) or be critical of men in private (Emilia),

TASK

Do you think the very different attitude to women in the early sixteenth century is responsible for the tragic events of the play? Could Iago have manipulated Othello so easily if Othello held more 'modern' views about women?

essentially they have no choice but to conform and comply on pain of rejection, violence or death. Desdemona learns not to complain and, with the psychology of the victim of domestic violence, begins to blame herself and make excuses for her abuser.

Male fantasies

In medieval and sixteenth-century literature, written by men, women tended to be represented as either Christian martyrs or malevolent devils, one extreme to the other (and this continued until the end of the nineteenth century). Characters divide women into virgins and saints, or whores and devils, with nothing in between; the former could become the latter overnight, but not vice versa. Women, as the unknowable 'other', could easily be the seen as the enemy and destroyer, pretending to be angels, but really in league with Satan to lure men to their doom through seduction and enchantment. Dialogues between all the male characters reveal a deep-seated fear of women deceiving them and thereby gaining supremacy and making them a laughing stock, as also revealed by Brabantio's dream, Cassio's reaction to the idea that Bianca wants him to marry her, and Othello's horror of cuckoldry.

Cultural context

The England of the early 1600s was involved in ambitious ventures of discovery and colonial expansion. The new century brought new challenges to the Elizabethan world view and ideology inherited from the Middle Ages, and this conflict is represented in the tragedy here. Below are some of the contemporary religious beliefs and social attitudes that throw light on the hopes, fears, thoughts and actions of the characters in *Othello*, and that Shakespeare exploits, while simultaneously calling them into question.

The chain of being

The Elizabethans inherited from medieval theology the idea of a hierarchical chain of being on which every creature appeared in its ordained position on a ladder descending from God through angel, king, man and woman (in that order), to animal, vegetable and finally mineral. It is necessary to know more about this belief in a divine order to appreciate the objection to women ruling men, and why it was believed that failure to apply reason reduced humans to the animal state of being governed by appetite and instinct alone. In Shakespeare, a human who falls below the level of man into bestiality is labelled a monster. Likewise, any change of reversal in this order is likely to result in tragedy.

Taking it further ▶▶

Research the chain of being. See if you can construct or draw a model of the hierarchical chain of being. Place the characters of *Othello* within this model of diagram. How does tragedy affect this order?

Nature

The ubiquitous presence of the word nature in Elizabethan literature, in addition to imagery deriving from it, and arguments about it, stems from the contemporary debate about the definition of nature, which has two contradictory aspects: the benign and harmonious, and the malignant and violent. Shakespeare's plays also examine closely the concept of human nature and its relationship to nature as a whole. Reversals of nature or what is 'natural' will inevitably invert the order and result in catastrophe.

Appearance

External appearance was believed by many in Shakespeare's time to be what lay within, that is, goodness or evil. Appearance versus reality is a central issue in *Othello*, and the imagery of' 'seeming' permeates the language of this and many other Shakespearean plays. If appearances, which are all we have to go on, are deceptive, and therefore character judgement is false, knowledge erroneous and truth elusive, then one cannot be sure of anything. This is the conundrum that torments many of Shakespeare's tragic heroes, because Iago looks honest, Othello assumes him incapable of villainy. This uncertainty over appearance is a more modern concept of identity, which the Elizabethans were only beginning to grasp – sometimes with tragic consequences.

Black and white

Black was traditionally the colour of evil and of the devil, according to Biblical and mythological sources. **'Fair'**, 'white' and other words were associated with light, which were part of a semantic field of beauty and goodness, whereas 'dark', 'dusky' and 'night' held the opposite connotations of ugliness and barbarism, which Iago is able to use to powerful effect against the 'sooty-bosomed' Moor. A marriage between a black man and a white woman – and the idea of their possible 'filthy' progeny – would have been deeply shocking at the time. When black and white absolutes shift position, the society might well expect tragic events to occur.

Top ten quotation

Reason

The failure of reason was considered to be the cause of the Fall of Man (Adam followed his love for Eve to overrule his better judgement and obedience to God), and Elizabethans therefore believed it was dangerous to let reason be dominated by passion. Characters in Shakespeare who became uncontrollably emotional are heading for a fall, as their intellect is what makes them human (superior to beasts) and keeps them sane. Othello gives way to his wrath and this is the downward turning point for him. In a state of heightened passion, such as anger and jealousy, mistakes are made, impulses are activated without sufficient reflection to moderate them, and one is no longer in control of oneself or the situation. A lack of reason will always lead to tragic consequences.

Evil spirits

Evil spirits were believed to be ever within earshot and on the watch for opportunity to corrupt and snatch a human soul from the pathway of righteousness. Characters in Shakespeare who are foolish, hubristic or tempted enough to invoke spirits from murky hell to help them commit foul deeds are sealing their own damnation (as both Iago and Othello do at 1.3.350–4 and 3.3.450 respectively). Othello fears this is what he has done in marrying Desdemona, and Brabantio in inviting Othello to his house. However, Othello's invitation to evil actually takes the form of him giving ear to Iago's temptations and bonding himself to him.

Damnation

The fear of damnation and of hell apparent in the works of Shakespeare and his fellow playwrights stems from the contemporary conviction that there literally was such a place below ground, inhabited by tormented souls allowed to walk the earth between midnight and dawn. Hell was typically portrayed the way Othello describes it, and engulfed in dark flames fuelled by sulphur (brimstone) to torture human flesh. The Elizabethans also believed in witches, diabolic possession and the incarnation of the devil and his agents in human form – which is how Othello finally sees Iago. The journey to hell is part of the tragic process.

Lying

Telling lies was a form of deception considered to be a much more serious offence then than nowadays. It was a diabolical trick because Satan told lies to Eve in the Garden of Eden. Telling the truth was the way to shame the devil, and lying meant putting one's soul at risk, especially since promises and oaths were thought to be witnessed by heaven. A gentleman's word was assumed to be the truth unless there was good reason to believe otherwise – which in Iago's case there is not – and it was a grave insult to call someone a liar.

Jealousy

Because irrational, jealousy was viewed as a sudden infection against which there was no prevention or cure. It eroded trust and dissolved the bonds holding together marriages, families and the social framework; it could let in evil and chaos. It guarantees calamity and tragedy.

Chaos

Shakespeare's contemporaries had a terror of a return to the anarchy of civil wars.

Chaos was the undoing of God's creation, a return to darkness and nothingness indicating the breakdown of the chain of being, the harmony of the universe, and nature's 'understood relations' (*Macbeth*). Shakespeare's contemporaries had a terror of the return of the anarchy of the civil wars period prior to the Tudor settlement and mostly peaceful reign of Elizabeth I. Chaos could initiate personal and civic tragedy.

Chaos meant more than just disorder, it was an image of a return to the state prior to the creation of the universe, that is, the black void. For chaos to come again the world must be de-created through a 'gross revolt' against nature – this is what Desdemona is accused of in her choice of husband by Iago, and in her lustfulness by Othello. The barrier against chaos is reason; Othello asks Iago for a reason, and is refused, the last time he speaks to him. Without a cause the universe makes no sense and madness and chaos rule.

Taking it further ▶

Research any one of the issues related to cultural context. Find examples of where they occur in other forms of literature or theatre, but also consider where they are placed within *Othello*.

Courtly love

Romance was the genre of courtly love, represented in *Othello* by Cassio, the attractive ladies' man with his chivalrous manners and poetic language, devoted to the fair lady, who he worships as a divinity. She is expected to have rival suitors for her hand, competing for the right to serve her. Romance concerned exotic tales of magic, superstition and travel to distant parts, as well as love affairs, and brought together the masculine ideals of the soldier and the lover, as in the Arthurian legends. By definition, the courtly lover had to be a member of high society and concerned above all with the notions of honour and reputation. Here however, the ideal of courtly love goes tragically wrong.

Cuckoldry

Cuckoldry, becoming a horned beast, was a prevalent male fear at the time, as it meant not only being an object of ridicule as a man who could not control his wife, and who had married a woman with unnatural sexual appetite, but was related to the wider issue of primogeniture and succession. Illegitimate children could not be assimilated comfortably into the family structure and were seen as a threat to the social fabric and the cause of inheritance complications and sibling resentments. Though desirable, young and beautiful wives were considered dangerous, as they were likely to both captivate their husbands and to be the target for seduction by other men, as Roderigo confirms. Cuckoldry may be seen as an initiator of tragedy.

Chastity

The insistence on female chastity in so many Shakespeare plays is because of the security of society and peace of mind of men was dependent upon women's virginity before marriage and chastity after it, meaning faithfulness to their husbands. In a society that passed inheritance down the male line, men needed to be sure that their son was really their own and not someone else's bastard, and a man's reputation would be destroyed by an unfaithful wife. This is why the issue of chastity is such a crucial lever to the plot of *Othello*.

Literary context

It is widely assumed that Shakespeare never left England, though the majority of his plays in all genres are set in other countries. Italy was particularly favoured, because it was the origin of the Renaissance and home to many source texts that inspired Shakespeare and his contemporaries. Foreign settings also have the advantage of allowing comment on home-grown political and social issues to be made circumspectly. Shakespeare wrote two plays set in Venice, a city of interest to London as a major trading rival, to which English merchants travelled and brought back reports of its luxuries and vices. Exaggerated travellers' tales were in vogue at the time *Othello* was written. This is the only Shakespeare play to be set roughly in its own time.

Shakespeare used known sources for 35 of his 37 plays, and it is assumed that the other two must have had sources as yet undiscovered. In this period, before and some time after (until the emergence of the aptly named 'novel' genre in the early eighteenth century in fact), originality of plot or character was not considered necessary or even desirable in literary works; a largely illiterate population and a traditional oral culture created a demand for the reassuringly familiar. Audiences expected to already know the basic storylines, settings and outcomes of the plays they attended, and the skill and creativity of the playwright was demonstrated by the quality of improvements made to an existing work, including the adaptation of the genre.

There is a particularly full and detailed source for *Othello*, namely Giraldi Cinthio's story – which may have been called 'El Capitano Moro' – in his collection of 100 tales called *Hecatommithi*, published in 1563 in Venice. There is not known to be an English translation until 1753, so Shakespeare may have read it either in Italian or in a French translation.

Comparing Shakespeare's play with its source makes it possible to appreciate *Othello* better. The list of statements below describing Cintho's version gives the main differences between the short story and the play.

- The only named character is Desdemona.
- Othello is only called 'The Moor'.
- There is no elopement.
- There is no Turkish threat.
- The couple travel on the same ship.
- Iago falls in love with Desdemona.
- Iago's sole motive is sexual jealousy of Cassio.
- Iago has no hatred of Othello.
- The murder plot is against Desdemona.
- There is no Roderigo.
- Desdemona's father is not mentioned specifically.

- Cassio does not suffer from drunkenness.
- Iago has a young daughter.
- Iago steals the handkerchief himself.
- Cassio recognises the handkerchief.
- Iago's wife knows the whole story.
- Iago and Othello kill Desdemona together.
- The murder is presented as an accident.
- The Moor is killed by Desdemona's kinsmen.
- Iago is tortured to death for another crime.

Taking it further ▷

Consider the implications of this early version of the story. Consider the reasons why you think Shakespeare made changes to the original narrative and how these may have improved the story.

The printed text

No manuscripts of Shakespeare's plays have survived. Some of the plays were published during his lifetime, in editions known as 'Quarto' from the size of paper used. After his death, a collected edition known as the First Folio was published in 1623, which contains all of his plays, except *Pericles*.

Othello was first published in quarto in 1622, six years after Shakespeare's death and just a year before the Folio. There are nevertheless significant differences between the two texts. Any decent edition will have an appendix discussing the textual problem, in which the editor will explain and justify the choice of text. The New Arden edition (ed. E.A.J. Honigmann, 1999) is principally based on the quarto; the New Penguin edition (ed. K. Muir, 1968) is based on the Folio.

The Folio is 168 lines longer than the quarto. We know that Shakespeare often revised the texts of his plays, and made deletions, and there is no consensus as to which is the more genuine or reliable text. Whichever edition you use, a number of changes will have been made from the original text. Different editors often have different views on and arrive at different conclusions. The changes, and arguments for them, are usually indicated in the textual notes, but generally, the goal of an editor is to produce an edition that makes sense when acted on the stage, rather than to give an account of all the possible interpretations of the play.

The Tragedy of Othello, the Moor of Venice

Othello (full title above) is one of the four great tragedies of the first decade of the seventeenth century and was probably written in 1603 (though a later date has been argued) but in any case before its performance in 1604, and between *Hamlet* (1600) and *King Lear* (1605). Honigmann, the editor of the Arden edition, believes it was inspired by the visit of the ambassador of the King of Barbary to

London in 1600–1, with his retinue known as the 'Barbarians', which was much discussed by Londoners at the time. Honigmann points out that also in 1600, a translation of John Leo's *A Geographic Historie of Africa* was published, in which Leo, a Moor brought up in Barbary, wrote about his fellow countrymen in terms very similar to the character traits of Othello. He called them 'honest', 'proud', 'high-minded', 'addicted unto wrath', 'credulous', 'subject unto jealousy', and willing to lose their lives rather than put up with disgrace on behalf of their women.

Othello has been called a tragedy of intrigue as opposed to a tragedy of revenge, a popular type of play at the time, though the two are related. Jealousy and cuckoldry were traditionally topics for comedy, and there are scenes in the play, notably the harbour scene and the street scenes, that are typical of this genre. Many of the characters are recognisable stereotypes from contemporary comedies, such as the gull (the fool, i.e. Roderigo), the senex (old man, i.e. Brabantio) and the clever, plotting slave (Iago). There is also a classic scene of comic cross-purposes (Cassio's supposed confession in Act 4, Scene 1), which can be compared to the scene in *Twelfth Night* when Antonio demands his purse from the wrong twin. The play employs two other comedy conventions: the 'contaminator (slanderer) believed' and the 'deceiver deceived'. What is daring about *Othello* is that comic devices enrich the tragedy by providing an alternative perspective on it, rather than by being juxtaposed with it, as in *Antony and Cleopatra*. In *Othello*, the ludicrous and risible are inseparable elements of the tragedy, which makes it the more poignant and ironic.

The play in performance

First performed at court in the autumn of 1604, *Othello* has been in continual production for 400 years — with constantly changing attitudes towards it and interpretations of it — and was originally one of the most popular Shakespeare plays. However, notions of refinement, decency and female sensibility meant that from the Restoration period to the recent past, performances of expurgated and abridged versions of the text were the norm, and this was particularly true in the eighteenth century, when the clown scenes, the character of Bianca, sexual language, Othello's fit and violence against Desdemona were all omitted. The willow scene (Act 4, Scene 3) is usually drastically cut, and justified on the grounds that the song is omitted from the quarto. Unjustifiable insertions have also been made to add to the tragic pathos, especially in the final scene.

More than any other Shakespeare play, *Othello* has caused controversy and audience reaction has been painfully intense. Unlike in *King Lear* and *Macbeth*, the killing of women takes place on stage, which creates a highly charged scene and a disturbing one for audiences. Spectators have frequently been driven to call out warnings and advice to Othello, and denunciations of Iago.

Race, costume and age are all questions affecting the portrayal of Othello. Shakespeare knew that Moors could be tawny-skinned if they came from the

Barbary north coast of Africa. Despite Roderigo's intended insult of 'thick lips', probably a racist exaggeration, it is likely that Othello is of lighter skin and colour than a Negro-black. As a proud Christian, it is unlikely that Othello would be dressed differently from the Venetians though the stage Moors of the plays performed in the 1590s, such as *The Spanish Moor's Tragedy*, wore turbans and carried scimitars to indicate religion and temperament. Although Othello is supposed to be a lot older than Desdemona (at least 20 years and probably 25), many productions cast them as equals in age. Another question for the actor/director is whether Othello should have a foreign accent (representing in English his non-native use of Italian).

Though a relatively short play (average 205 minutes), it is very emotionally and physically demanding on the actor playing Othello, particularly during his seizure in Act 4, Scene 1. He has to manifest extreme behaviour and passion throughout the second half of the play, and it has been known for actors to fall ill. There have been two kinds of Othello over the years: the dignified, lyrical and sensitive versus the passionate, sensual and violent. Richard Burbage, the leading actor in Shakespeare's company, first played the part of the Moor, and his performance was considered deeply moving and acclaimed as one of his greatest successes. Other notable Othellos over the centuries have been Thomas Betterton in the early eighteenth century, Edwin Booth, a refined and polished Moor in the nineteenth century, Tomaso Salvini, who made animal noises and movements, was tempestuous, spoke his lines in Italian and was the first Othello to strike Desdemona, and Laurence Olivier, who stressed his race and sexuality, and gave an 'outlandish vocal performance' (Arden introduction 2002, p. 28).

Iago is on stage in nearly every scene and therefore he is under pressure and the scrutiny of the audience almost continuously. He must not look or behave like an obvious villain, or this would destroy his credibility and the point the play is making about the unrecognisability of evil. The crucial thing for an actor to get right is Iago's body language and facial expressions, and to find the balance between his being a damaged human and diabolically powerful. Actors complain that motivelessness is unactable, and that Shakespeare himself 'has not got a clear line on Iago'. It is interesting that so many famous actors through the centuries have tried their skills in the roles of both Othello and Iago, even switching alternate nights in some cases.

Desdemonas have to decide how passive to be in their delivery, tone and movements. For instance, does she stay in bed in Act 5, Scene 2 or try to escape from her psychopathic husband when she realises his intent? Is she completely innocent and naive or does she deliberately put on a girlish and flirtatious act to get her own way? Minor characters also give scope for varying and even opposite interpretations. Roderigo, for instance, is usually played as a comic character, fooled and mocked by Iago, and held in contempt by the audience for his weakness and gullibility, but the Oliver Parker film (1995) portrays him as a dangerous and explosive character driven to more desperate and violent acts.

TASK

Iago is on stage for most of the play. In the few moments where we do not see him, what do you imagine him to be doing?

CRITICAL VIEW

In 1692, *Othello* was attacked in the 'hysterical criticism' of the notorious Thomas Rymer for its improbability, its lack of justice and its character assassination of common soldiers; the character of Iago was deemed incredible because soldiers (he thought) were genuinely honest. It was also interpreted by Rymer, and others later, as a warning to maidens not to run away with blackamoors and to take better care of their linen.

Our interpretations should include responses to the issues that concern us.

The tempo of the play is fast, sustained and tightly plotted, with many scenes starting *in medias res* (Latin for 'in the middle of things'). There is no redundancy, recapitulation, change of action focus or use of peripheral characters as there are in the other major tragedies — particularly when directors omit, as they often do, the two short clown scenes (3.1.3–29 and 3.4.1–22). The audience, similar to Othello and Desdemona's emotions and reputations, is subjected to continuous 'verbal mugging' (Arden introduction, p. 64). There is continuous tension from Act 3 onwards, to the extent that it is difficult to find a place for an interval; the only place, logically, is between Acts 3 and 4, but this destroys the dramatic intensity of Iago's verbal assault upon Othello and a break here is anticlimactic.

If the reward for innocence is brutal death, then the play can be seen as immoral. This particularly bothered critics in the eighteenth century, and Samuel Johnson admitted to finding the final scene in *Othello* as unendurable.

Shakespeare's achievement with the tragedies was not fully appreciated until the Romantic period, when analysis of psychological states and human relationships became the focus of critical interest. Coleridge was an influential critic who responded intuitively and sensitively to the emotions being explored through the medium of the main characters, and who coined the famous phrase about Iago's 'motiveless malignity'. The play remained popular throughout the nineteenth century, with Iago's character at the centre of literary debate. To the present day critics are divided over the extent to which they consider Othello to blame, and over whether Othello redeems himself in any way at the end. T.S. Eliot thought not. Bradley found the play depressing, and Granville-Barker declared it a tragedy without meaning.

A variety of criticism

Any play must be considered in relation to the historical, social, political, economic and religious background that produced it, and be reviewed in the context of contemporary attitudes. On the other hand, our critical interpretations should include responses to issues that concern us nowadays, such as the stereotyping of race and gender in the portrayal of black people and women. Recent critical approaches that are relevant to the study of *Othello* include:

- *Feminist criticism*: This tries to ascertain whether the play challenges or accepts and endorses the patriarchal ideology and misogyny of its time.
- *Post-colonial criticism*: This studies the way Othello is perceived as the 'other' in a white world.
- *Structuralist criticism*: This looks at language to expose the shifting and ambivalent relationship between words and meaning (signifier and signified).
- *Post-structural criticism*: This looks for what is not there as well as what is, at how the plot is framed and at the assumptions being made.

- *Psychoanalytical criticism*: This seeks to expose and interpret images and repressed desires; these become the symbols that construct personal and social identities.

- *Marxist criticism*: This addresses the politics of the world outside of the text to show how literature is governed by a set of socioeconomic beliefs and assumptions that distort the presentation of social reality.

- *New historicist criticism*: This rejects the autonomy of the author and the literary work, and sees both as inseparable from the broader historical context. The literary text is part of a wider cultural, political, social, economic and religious framework, which determines the morals of authors and of characters.

- *Cultural materialist criticism*: Similar to new historicism, this focuses on the role of ideology and institutions in the construction of identity, and on the potential for dissidence; it is particularly interested in groups marginalised by society.

- *Presentist criticism*: This believes that the consumption of texts in the present is paramount, and the only way of making literary criticism directly relevant to the 'now'.

A combination of all these approaches will produce examination answers that show an awareness of a range of reader responses and audience reactions, and that cover examination assessment criteria.

Assessment objectives and skills

The five key English literature assessment objectives (AOs) describe the different skills you need to show in order to succeed in the examination. Regardless of what texts or what examination specification you are following, the AOs lie at the heart of your study of English literature at AS and A2; they let you know exactly what the examiners are looking for and provide a helpful framework for your literary studies.

The assessment objectives require you to:

AO1	Articulate, informed, personal and creative responses to literary texts, using appropriate terminology and concepts, and coherent, accurate written expression.
AO2	Analyse the ways in which meanings are shaped in literary texts.
AO3	Demonstrate understanding of the significance and influence of the contexts in which literary texts are written and received.
AO4	Explore connections across different literary texts.
AO5	Explore literary texts informed by different interpretations.

Try to bear in mind that the AOs are there to support rather than restrict you; don't look at them as encouraging a tick-box approach or a mechanistic and reductive way into the study of literature. Examination questions are written with the AOs in mind, so if you answer them clearly and carefully you should automatically hit the right targets. If you are devising your own questions for coursework, seek the help of your teacher to ensure that your essay title is worded in such a way that it addresses the required assessment objectives.

Also, remember that the AOs do not operate in isolation. You should expect them to overlap, so that in dealing with any one element of the text you may well be addressing more than one AO.

Although the assessment objectives are common to all the exam boards, each specification varies in the way they meet the requirements. The boards' websites provide useful information, including sections for students, past papers, sample papers and mark schemes.

- AQA: www.aqa.org.uk
- EDEXCEL: www.edexcel.com
- OCR: www.ocr.org.uk
- WJEC: www.wjec.co.uk

Remember, although you need to address the skills outlined in the assessment objectives, the focus of your answer will always be the text. There is no substitute for having a thorough, well-informed knowledge of the text.

> **AO1** Articulate, informed, personal and creative responses to literary texts, using appropriate terminology and concepts, and coherent, accurate written expression.

- AO1 requires you to set out and explain your ideas about the text in a clear, accurate and well-structured way.

- It is extremely important that the material you choose is relevant to the question. One of the marks of good writing is the ability to distinguish what is directly relevant from what is only very indirectly connected to the task. It is often the case that when candidates have not performed up to expectation the reason is that they have failed to directly address the requirements of the task. AO1 rewards sustained focus on the subject of the task.

- For this reason, a very important skill is learning to read the questions carefully. These are not designed to trick you, but will be phrased very precisely, and it is important that you consider the implications of every part of the question.

- The form of your response will be driven by the requirements of the examination. How you organise your writing will in part depend on the time you have available. NEA (coursework) responses are likely to involve more extended writing, and should benefit from the conditions under which you produce the work. There is less excuse for technical error when there is so much time available to proofread what you have written.

- A very important part of any essay or other form of writing is the opening paragraph. This will be what makes the first impression on the reader, and should establish the ground on which you are going to build during the remainder of your response. There is little point in offering nothing more than a basic restatement of the task. There should be something in the opening paragraph for an examiner to credit, some point you are making in relation to the task or the text or both.

- Your argument then needs to be developed. You need to connect the different parts of your discussion with care, ensuring that each paragraph follows naturally from what has gone before, while also signalling the relevance of your material. Look carefully at the opening sentences of every paragraph. Do they clearly connect your developing argument with the key words of the task?

- Avoid conclusions that simply restate what you have already said, but in a less interesting way. Do, however, bring your writing to a firm end, in which some final point is made.

▼ Sustained close references to the text matter. These are not optional extras, but will be expected of you whether the examination is open or closed book. When studying *Othello*, you will need to be able to quote directly from the speeches in the play. The most effective quotations are often brief and embedded in your own sentences (e.g. *In his soliloquy at the end of Act 2, Iago's references to 'hell', 'devils' and 'sin' help to reveal his diabolic nature.*). Quotations need to be as accurate as possible and not merely as decorations to the argument, but clearly used in support of the points you are making.

> **AO2** Analyse the ways in which meanings are shaped in literary texts.

▼ AO2 requires you to explore the craft of the writer. With *Othello* you will be looking at the various ways in which Shakespeare shapes meanings through his dramatic methods. How does he manage the story that he tells?

▼ An important aspect of dramatic method is dramatic structure. One obvious way in which *Othello* is structured is through the act and scene divisions, but it is also worth looking at wider and narrower aspects of structure within the play, including changing settings of time and place, the pattern of appearances of different characters and the internal structure of individual speeches.

▼ You will also want to look at form, the type of text you are studying. With *Othello*, this will involve looking at the play <u>as</u> a play, and also as an example of dramatic tragedy.

▼ The different voices within the play also need to be analysed. Here you might be looking at the different kinds of dramatic language within the play, the contrasts between different characters, and the contrasting kinds of language that we observe within the speeches of one individual character.

> **AO3** Demonstrate understanding of the significance and influence of the contexts in which literary texts are written and received.

▼ AO3 focuses on the significance and influence of the contexts in which literary texts are written and received.

▼ The context of reception is at least as important as the context of production. For instance, you need to be very careful about offering broad generalisations about what an audience in Shakespeare's time <u>would</u> think or feel. What you certainly can consider is the significance of major cultural and social differences between the original contemporary context of production and the twenty-first century context in which you receive the text. General historical developments and important changes in attitudes to race suggest that a modern audience is unlikely to respond to *Othello* in the same way as a seventeenth-century audience. Looking at the stage history of the play is an interesting way of exploring these changing attitudes.

▼ Remember that there are a range of relevant contexts that you might consider in relation to the play. Historical or biographical material are not always the most productive areas for analysis. Cultural or literary contexts are often equally or even more important. To access AO3 successfully you might have to think about how any of the contexts of production, reception, literature, culture, biography, geography, society, history, genre and intertextuality can affect texts.

▼ Any selection of contextual material must be directly relevant to the task you have been given. The fact that the material you have chosen is accurate in terms of the facts does not mean that it necessarily helps or advances your argument. Examiners will not be impressed by a clumsy bolted-on rehash of a website or some notes that you have copied from a textbook. Examiners want to see a selective sense of contextual relevance woven into the fabric of your essay.

▼ The text must remain the central focus of your response to the task. Don't allow contextual material to drift away from the text and become its own self-justification.

▼ It is quite possible that there will be an overlap between contexts and interpretations, so don't worry about separating out the AOs here (and elsewhere).

AO4   Explore connections across different literary texts.

▼ AO4 requires you to explore different connections between literary texts.

▼ These connections can take many forms, but connections in terms of genre are always likely to be very important. If you are considering some of the features of dramatic tragedy that appear within *Othello*, for instance, you are implicitly connecting the text with all the other plays that fall within that genre.

▼ If you make a more direct connection between *Othello* and another named text, the connection must genuinely illuminate your analysis, and make a point about *Othello* that could not be so well established through other means. The reference to another text should not be merely a means of demonstrating your ability to make wider reference, particularly if you have only limited knowledge of the 'other' text in question.

▼ Connections between texts in terms of authorial method may be as interesting and productive as connections in terms of content or 'theme'.

▼ Remember that differences between texts may often be as illuminating as perceived similarities.

▼ When writing comparatively, use words and constructions that will help you to link your texts, such as 'whereas', 'on the other hand', 'while', 'in contrast', 'by comparison', 'as in', 'differently', 'similarly', 'comparably'.

> **AO5**   Explore literary texts informed by different interpretations.

- AO5 asks you to look at the different ways that texts can be interpreted. It is based on the idea that any text is at certain points naturally open to different readings.
- You need to measure your interpretation of a text against that of other readers.
- These other readings may emerge from classroom or lecture room discussion, or from critical opinions that you have read or heard elsewhere.
- Although the views of a named critic may be a useful way of broadening your argument, it is not the case that examiners will judge the quality of your work by the number of critics you can name in the course of your essay.
- Always be prepared to challenge and question a given view; there is nothing more dispiriting for an examiner than to read a set of scripts from one centre that all say exactly the same thing. The best candidates produce fresh personal responses rather than merely regurgitating the ideas of others, however famous or insightful their interpretations may be.
- Your use of critical readings needs to be embedded within your own argument. Uncritical reference to critical views will only get you so far. Work towards or around the selected reading of the text in your discussion, instead of allowing your own views to hang limply from the quoted opinions of others.
- Another way of exploring different readings of a text is to apply general critical perspectives: e.g. Marxist, feminist, new historicist, post-structuralist, psychoanalytic, or eco-critical.
- Try to show an awareness of multiple readings with regard to your chosen text and an understanding that the meaning of a text is dependent as much upon what the reader brings to it as what the writer left there. Using modal verb phrases such as 'may be seen as', 'might be interpreted as' or 'could be represented as' implies that you are aware that different readers interpret texts in different ways at different times. The key word here is plurality; there is no single meaning, no right answer, and you need to evaluate a range of other ways of making textual meanings as you work towards your own.
- Remember that whatever critical reading of the text you consider, it must be relevant to the task, not used simply because you have committed it to memory.

Taking it further ▶▶

The Casebook on Othello, edited by John Wain, gives examples of interpretations by different readers over time.

Examinations

Examination essay questions

1 A-level English Literature AQA B

'At the end of the play, Othello fails to regain any honour and nobility.'

To what extent do you agree with this view?

Top band answers to this question demonstrated the following features:

AO1	• Perceptive, assured and sophisticated argument in relation to the task • Assured use of literary critical concepts and terminology; mature and impressive expression • A well-structured and well-informed argument focusing on the changes in Othello's language and actions during the play, and in particular on the final scenes • Fluent, coherent and accurate writing • Sustained and appropriate textual reference
AO2	• Perceptive understanding of authorial methods in relation to the task • Assured engagement with how meanings are shaped by the methods used • Particular attention paid to Othello's speeches and actions in the final scenes, with wider reference to how Othello is presented in the earlier part of the play
AO3	• Perceptive understanding of the significance of relevant contexts in relation to the task • Assuredness in the connection between those contexts and the genre studied • Confident treatment of the concepts of 'honour' and 'nobility' as represented in the world of the play
AO4	• Perceptive exploration of connections across literary texts arising out of generic study • Assured and perceptive exploration of relevant elements of dramatic tragedy
AO5	• Perceptive and confident engagement with the debate set up in the task • Clearly developed judgements well informed by an appreciation of different possible readings of the text

Note the repetition of the two key terms 'perceptive' and 'assured'. You will demonstrate 'perception' when your response shows deep understanding and a discriminating selection of material. You will demonstrate 'assuredness' when your writing is confident, consistent and sophisticated. Top band writing often has flashes of independent and individual insight into the text.

A top band response to this question would demand careful and selective treatment of the ways Othello might appear to an audience at the beginning of the play, and a discriminating examination of the evidence of the final scenes. A debate is possible between a reading of the play that sees Othello as regaining some greatness of spirit in his final moments and another reading that might regard his rhetoric and actions much less positively.

2 A-level English Literature AQA A

'Typically, texts about love present the feelings of love and duty as often connected and often in opposition.'

In the light of this view, discuss how Shakespeare presents attitudes to love and duty in this extract (4.3.1–77) and elsewhere in the play.

Top band answers to this question demonstrated the following features:

AO1	• Perceptive, assured and sophisticated argument in relation to the task • Assured use of literary critical concepts and terminology; mature and impressive expression • A well-structured and well-informed argument focusing on the concepts of love and duty within in the play • Fluent, coherent and accurate writing • Sustained and appropriate textual reference
AO2	• Perceptive understanding of authorial methods in relation to the task • Assured engagement with how meanings are shaped by the methods used • Particular attention paid to how the different attitudes towards love and duty are presented in the play
AO3	• Perceptive understanding of the significance of relevant contexts in relation to the task • Assuredness in the connection between those contexts and the genre studied • Confident treatment of the concepts of 'love' and 'duty' as represented in the world of the play. In exploring these concepts, top band students will engage with the contexts of when the text was written and how it has been received
AO4	• Perceptive exploration of connections across literary texts arising out of the love through the ages theme • Assured and perceptive exploration of relevant elements of dramatic tragedy • Students might consider the significance of the domestic and public worlds within the play, and the degree to which *Othello* can be seen as a domestic tragedy • Students might focus on typical representations of love and duty in other texts and the degree to which these feelings collide
AO5	• Perceptive and confident engagement with the debate set up in the task • Clearly developed judgements well informed by an appreciation of different possible readings of the text • Students might explore the very different attitudes to love and duty displayed by the different characters in the play, or the ways in which Desdemona is torn between different duties

Note the repetition of the two key terms 'perceptive' and 'assured'. You will demonstrate 'perception' when your response shows deep understanding and a discriminating selection of material. You will demonstrate 'assuredness' when your writing is confident, consistent and sophisticated. Top band writing often has flashes of independent and individual insight into the text.

A top band response to this question would demand careful and selective treatment of the different ways love and duty are presented in the play.

Important distinctions might be made between Iago's bitter and cynical references to love and duty and the more conventional views shown by Cassio. A debate is possible between a reading of *Othello* that argues that love and duty are ultimately celebrated in the play and a reading that sees these human feelings exposed as fragile and vulnerable.

3 A Level English Literature Edexcel

Explore Shakespeare's presentation of jealousy in *Othello*.

You must relate your discussion to relevant contextual factors and ideas from your critical reading.

Top band answers to this question demonstrated the following features:

AO1	<ul><li>Perceptive, assured and sophisticated argument in relation to the task</li><li>Assured use of literary critical concepts and terminology; mature and impressive expression</li><li>A well-structured and well-informed argument focusing on the concept of jealousy within in the play</li><li>Fluent, coherent and accurate writing</li><li>Sustained and appropriate textual reference</li></ul>
AO2	<ul><li>Perceptive and critical evaluation of authorial methods in relation to the task</li><li>Assured engagement with how meanings are shaped by the methods used</li><li>Particular attention paid to how the different attitudes towards jealousy are presented in the play</li></ul>
AO3	<ul><li>Sophisticated evaluation and appreciation of the significance of relevant contexts in relation to the task</li><li>Assuredness in the connection between those contexts and the text</li><li>Confident treatment of the concept of jealousy as represented in the world of the play. In exploring this concept, top band students will engage with the contexts of when the text was written and how it has been received.</li></ul>
AO5	<ul><li>Clearly developed judgements well informed by a sustained evaluation of different possible readings of the text</li><li>Sophisticated use of application of alternative interpretations to illuminate own critical position</li></ul>

Note the repetition of the two key terms **'perceptive'** and **'assured'**. You will demonstrate 'perception' when your response shows deep understanding and a discriminating selection of material. You will demonstrate 'assuredness' when your writing is confident, consistent and sophisticated. Top band writing often has flashes of independent and individual insight into the text.

A top band response to this question would demand careful and selective treatment of the different ways jealousy is presented in the play. Productive references might be made to the different forms of jealousy shown by Othello, Iago and Bianca. A debate is possible between a reading of *Othello* that argues that sexual jealousy is the central driving force in the play and a reading which argues that other kinds of jealousy are equally significant.

Some interpretations of the play that you might use for discussion or adapt for essay practice:

1 'It is essential to the development of the play's tragic situation that Othello, Iago and Cassio are soldiers.'

2 'Both Othello's jealousy itself and the speed with which it develops are absurd.'

3 '*Othello* is a tragedy without meaning and that is the ultimate horror of it'.

4 Wilson Knight said 'Othello loves emotion for its own sake, luxuriates in it'.

5 'The enduring interest of the play is its treatment of race and the outsider'.

6 'The great failing of *Othello* is that Desdemona and Emilia are too weak and easily deceived to be convincing.'

7 'The real tragedy of the play is that Othello proves that the world really is as Iago sees it.'

8 Bradley says of Iago, 'He is the spirit of denial of all romantic values'.

9 Leavis claimed that 'Othello is too stupid to be regarded as a tragic hero'.

10 '*Othello* is the tale of a gullible hero deceived by a melodramatic villain.'

Building skills 1: Structuring your writing

This section focuses upon organising your written responses to convey your ideas as clearly and effectively as possible: the 'how' of your writing as opposed to the 'what'. More often than not, if your knowledge and understanding of *Othello* is sound, a disappointing mark or grade will be down to one of two common mistakes: misreading the question or failing to organise your response economically and effectively.

Understanding your examination

It's important to prepare for the specific type of response your examination body sets with regard to *Othello*. You need to know if your paper is **open book** – that is, you will have a clean copy of the text available to you in the exam, or **closed book**, in which case you won't. It is important that you find out about this, because the format of your assessment has major implications for the way you organise your response and dictates the depth and detail required to achieve a top band mark.

Open book

In an open book exam, when you have a copy of *Othello* on the desk in front of you, there can be no possible excuse for failing to quote relevantly, accurately and extensively. To gain a high mark you are expected to focus in detail on specific passages. Remember, too, that you must not refer to any supporting material such as the introduction notes contained within the set edition of your text. If an examiner suspects that you have been lifting chunks of unacknowledged material from such a source, they will refer your paper to the examining body for possible plagiarism.

Closed book

In a closed book exam, because the examiner is well aware that you do not have your text in front of you, their expectations will be different. While you are still expected to support your argument with relevant quotations, close textual references are also encouraged and rewarded. Again, since you will have had to memorise quotations, slight inaccuracies will not be severely punished. Rather than a forensically detailed analysis of a specific section of *Othello*, the examiner will expect you to range more broadly across the play to structure your response.

Extract-based questions

Writing about *Othello* in an extract-based examination question poses a very different set of challenges. You will need to ensure that your analysis of the given extract makes relevant wider reference to the text and task. It is almost certainly better to weave your wider references into your treatment of the extract rather than try to separate your response into comment on a) the extract and b) the play as a whole. As always, check that your analysis focuses on the central demands of the task.

Step 1: Planning and beginning: locate the debate

A very common type of exam question invites you to open up a debate about the text by using various trigger words and phrases such as **'consider the view that …'**, **'some readers think that …'** or **'how far do you agree with this view?'** When analysing this type of question, the one thing you can be sure of is that exam questions never offer a view that makes no sense at all or one so blindingly obvious that all anyone can do is agree with it; there will always be a genuine interpretation at stake. Your introduction needs to address the terms of this debate and sketch out how you intend to move the argument forward to orientate the reader. Since it's obviously going to be helpful if you actually know this before you start writing, you really do need to plan before you begin to write. It is worth experimenting with different forms of plan to see which work best for you. Bullet point lists or concept maps are two possibilities.

Undertaking a lively debate about some of the ways in which *Othello* has been and can be interpreted is the DNA of your essay. Of course any good argument needs to be honest but to begin by writing 'yes, I totally agree with this obviously true statement' suggests a fundamental misunderstanding of what studying literature is all about. Any stated view in an examination question is designed to open up critical conversations, not shut them down.

Plan your answer by collecting together points for and against the given view. Aim to see a stated opinion as an interesting way of exploring a key facet of *Othello*, as the following student does.

Student A

This sample comes from an answer to the following possible task from AQA Specification A Paper 1:

Othello, Act 1, Scene 3, 175–221

'Women in dramatic tragedies are presented as mere victims of love.'

How far do you agree, with direct reference to the dramatic presentation of Desdemona in this scene and elsewhere in *Othello*?

Shakespeare's tragedy, Othello, presents a story of inter-racial love, involving both victims and villains. The character of Desdemona, however, is so complex that an audience is discouraged from confidently placing her into the category of victim, either of love or anything else. It should be noted that Desdemona's behaviour alters during the course of the play; she changes from being a courageous, independently-minded woman into a submissive victim. It can be argued that — driven by Othello's fury and jealousy — she consciously chooses to play the role of a victim, rather than being forced into this role by other characters. In this respect, she resembles other fictional females such as Thomas Hardy's Tess and Emily Brontë's Catherine Earnshaw, both of whom can be seen as partially responsible for their own fate.

Her entrance in Act 1, Scene 3 presents Desdemona as both courageous and rebellious. She quickly attracts the attention of the audience, through her confident address to her father:

My noble father, I do perceive here a divided duty.

… you are the lord of duty,

I am hitherto your daughter. But here's my husband.

The fact that Desdemona addresses her father as 'the lord of duty', reflects the position young women would have occupied in regard to their fathers within the patriarchal Jacobean society of the time. The words 'divided duty' indicate Desdemona's awareness of the customs of the time; the active role she takes in her marriage, however, subverts contemporary gender roles. 'Here's my husband', she says, asserting the primacy of her loyalty to Othello. Briefly at this point in the play she dominates the stage, and the subsequent responses of Brabantio and the Duke attest to the impact of her words. Living in the predominately white society of Venice, and wooed by 'the wealthy curled darlings of our nation', she has nevertheless chosen to marry a black foreigner.

Examiner's commentary

This student:

- Immediately establishes a clear and sustained connection with the task **(AO1)** through selective use of key words (e.g. 'victims') and perceptive attention to aspects of dramatic presentation **(AO2)**.

- Uses quotations succinctly and incorporates them clearly into the argument **(AO1)**.

- Explores the ways that dramatic methods shape meanings within the text **(AO2)** through references to structure, stage entrances and patterns of dialogue.

- Clearly establishes the direction of a debate around readings of the play **(AO5)** through pointed use of discourse markers in the opening paragraph; this is confident, assured writing.

- Selects a relevant point of connection between texts **(AO4)** through the concept of being a victim of love.

▼ Incorporates into the argument carefully selected contextual references **(AO3)** to contemporary attitudes regarding nationhood and the duties of daughters.

If the rest of this essay maintains this level of performance, it is likely that this student will be on course to achieve a notional grade A.

Student B

This sample also comes from an answer to the following possible examination task from AQA A specification:

Othello Act 1, Scene 3, 175–221

Women in dramatic tragedies are presented as mere victims of love. How far do you agree, with direct reference to the dramatic presentation of Desdemona in this scene and elsewhere in *Othello*?

Desdemona is one of the three women in the play who are victims of love. She seems often to be powerless and completely under the influence of her father and her husband. Shakespeare shows that she is a victim by first revealing the image of a young and eager woman and then breaking down this image through Iago's spiteful plans and Othello's jealousy.

In Act 1, Scene 3, she shows her braveness in standing up to her father on behalf of Othello, but the 'duty' she shows here will later lead to her death. Emilia also shows love and duty to her husband, but these feelings will also lead to destruction, hers and Desdemona's. Bianca in a sense is also a victim of love. It is not quite clear if she suffers death at the end of the play, but she probably suffers punishment of some sort, and all this is due to her passion for Cassio. In The Great Gatsby Daisy can also be seen as a victim of love for her husband and Gatsby.

In Act 1, Scene 3, it could be argued that Desdemona is not wholly a victim as she shows courage in front of the Senate when she declares her love for Othello and shows that she was 'half the wooer' as her father asks her to.

Examiner's commentary

This student:

▼ Responds in a straightforward way to the task.

▼ Offers material that is relevant, but not particularly well-shaped; the argument drifts from Desdemona to Emilia and Bianca and back again without showing any clear direction **(AO1)**.

- Refers to 'images' but without any clear explanation of how these are presented **(AO2)**.
- Refers to incidents within the play, but fails to offer effective textual support.
- Offers some brief and undeveloped indication of connections between texts through the concept of being a victim of love **(AO4)**.
- Makes some reference to the dynamics of father–daughter relationships **(AO3)**.
- Offers some understanding that a debate is possible about the degree of Desdemona's victimhood **(AO5)**.

If the rest of this essay maintains this level of performance, it is likely that this student would be on course to achieve a notional grade C or D.

Step 2: Developing and linking – go with the flow

An essay is a very specific type of formal writing that requires an appropriate discourse structure. In the main body of your writing, you need to thread your developing argument through each paragraph consistently and logically, referring back to the terms established by the question itself, rephrasing and reframing as you go. It can be challenging to sustain the flow of your essay and keep firmly on track, but here are some techniques to help you:

- Ensure your essay doesn't disintegrate into a series of disconnected building blocks by creating a neat and stable bridge between one paragraph and the next.
- Use discourse markers – linking words and phrases like 'on the other hand', 'however', 'although' and 'moreover' – to hold the individual paragraphs of your essay together and signpost the connections between different sections of your overarching argument.
- Having set out an idea in Paragraph A, in Paragraph B you might need to then support it by providing a further example; if so, signal this to the reader with a phrase, such as: **'Moreover**, *this imagery of entrapment can also be seen when…'*
- To change direction and challenge an idea begun in Paragraph A by acknowledging that it is open to interpretation, you could begin Paragraph B with something like: **'On the other hand**, *this view of the play could be challenged by a feminist critic…'*
- Another typical paragraph-to-paragraph link is when you want to show that the original idea doesn't give the full picture. Here you could modify your original point with something like: **'Although** *it is possible to see Iago's comments as simply racist, this view does not take account of the social context of the 1600s, when a black man's marriage to a white woman would have been very unusual'.*

Student C

This sample comes from an answer to the following possible task from the Edexcel A-level English Literature specification.

To what extent does Shakespeare's *Othello* offer a sense of redemption at the end of the play? Relate your discussion to relevant contextual factors and critical readings.

Othello undergoes a great downfall where he becomes a victim of Iago's machinations and is caught up in his web of lies. His final, slightly oxymoronic, description of himself as 'an honourable murderer' might be seen by an audience as an example of a tragic hero justifying his actions, but the memory of his murder of his innocent wife is likely to cast a shadow. It should also be remembered that the protagonist might have been seen as a barbarian by an Elizabethan audience who were wary of other ethnic groups to their own. Modern audiences may be more sympathetic to Othello in his downfall.

It could also be argued that Othello's final act of suicide, being also an act of justice, offers some redemption. By delivering justice upon himself in the most severe way, Othello can be seen to have fully repented for his sins. He compares himself to 'a malignant and a turbaned Turk' who 'traduced the state' and whom Othello killed, as he now kills himself. This might be seen as a final act of service to the state of Venice, the state to which he has dedicated his life. A.C. Bradley has suggested that Othello is always conscious of his high position, and this connects him to other tragic heroes of 'high degree'.

However, his suicide might also be seen as a cowardly act, carried out to escape the 'cunning cruelty' that lies in wait for Iago. His words to Iago, ''tis happiness to die', suggest that he sees death as almost a release from suffering. But there is also evidence that he anticipates suffering eternal damnation for what was seen by Christians as the worst of crimes, suicide. He has already anticipated that 'fiends will snatch at' his soul for his murder of his wife. An audience is therefore likely to be caught between conflicting feelings about Othello's redemption at the end of the play.

Examiner's commentary

This student:

◤ Shapes the argument coherently, establishing clear links between the paragraphs through well-chosen discourse markers such as 'also' and 'however' **(A01)**; the discussion has pace and direction.

◤ The student moves from a consideration of the significance of the act of murder to Othello's suicide, maintaining close connection with the overarching task.

◤ Textual reference **(A01)** is sustained and appropriate; the student ranges effectively around the play and looks at aspects of dramatic language **(A02)**.

◤ **A03** is addressed through a consideration of the contexts of morality, religion and society; the reference to the contexts of production and reception offers opportunity for a debate around interpretations **(A05)**. Precise reference is made to ideas from the Edexcel *Critical Anthology*.

◤ Connections between *Othello* and other texts **(A04)** are established through the treatment of aspects of dramatic tragedy.

If the rest of this essay maintains this level of performance, this student should be on course to achieve a mark that equates to an A grade.

Student D

This sample also comes from an answer to the following possible task from the Edexcel English Literature A-level specification.

To what extent does Shakespeare's *Othello* offer a sense of redemption at the end of the play? Relate your discussion to relevant contextual factors and critical readings.

The audience changes their feelings towards Othello as the play develops and Iago begins to gain control. In the opening scenes the audience believe that Othello is an evil sort of man who is arrogant and too fond of himself, 'loving his own pride and purposes'. In the next act, though, we see that he is likeable and brave and honest. His speech is very romantic 'O my soul's joy' which suggests that he loves Desdemona and Iago's previous words had been lies.

This links to the lies that Iago continues to tell 'make the net that shall enmesh them' and foreshadows the play as he is influencing how the other characters act and think. The way Othello was described at the beginning of the play becomes true so the audience starts to fear Othello as much as respect him.

Othello becomes the character Iago wants him to be and suffers because of this, 'goats and monkeys!' Bradley says this is typical of tragedy when suffering affects a conspicuous person.

At the end, Shakespeare creates a mood of pity for Othello as he reveals that he was really a loving and admirable character who got caught up in Iago's plans. Othello tragically realises that he should not have trusted Iago. Othello was the tragic hero in the play so the audience would be sympathetic towards him because of all the pain and lies he has been through.

Examiner's commentary

This student:

- Selects some relevant material – reference to Iago's manipulation and how this might affect our view of Othello, for instance, but the focus on redemption at the end of the play is unclear. Tighter focus on the task is needed to improve this response.
- The connections between the paragraphs are loose: there is little effective cohesion here **(AO1)**.
- At times expression is imprecise: 'evil sort of man', and there is some uncritical assertion: 'the audience believe that…'
- Reference is made to aspects of Othello's language 'his speech is very romantic', but the quotation is not very illuminating **(AO2)**. Closer attention to the effect of words such as 'soul' in connection with his feelings would have improved this reference. More could have been made of the brief reference to aspects of structure in the first paragraph.
- There is reference to the views of the critic A.C. Bradley in the Edexcel *Critical Anthology* **(AO5)** and connections are made with other dramatic tragedies **(AO4)**.
- There is some straightforward reference to moral contexts **(AO3)**, but little developed material.

If the rest of this response reached this level of performance, this student should be on course to achieve a mark that equates to a notional C or D grade.

Step 3: Concluding: seal the deal

As you bring your writing to a close, you need to capture and clarify your response to the given view and make a relatively swift and elegant exit. Keep your final paragraph short and sweet. Now is not the time to introduce any new points – but equally, don't just reword everything you have already just said either. Potential closers include:

◤ looping the last paragraph back to something you mentioned in your introduction to suggest that you have now said all you have to say on the subject

◤ reflecting on your key points in order to reach a balanced overview

◤ ending with a punchy quotation that leaves the reader thinking

◤ discussing the contextual implications of the topic you have debated

◤ stating why you think the main issue, theme or character under discussion is so central to the play

◤ mentioning how different audiences over time might have responded to the topic you have been debating.

Student E

This task comes from an answer to the following possible task from AQA Specification B Paper 1.

Othello **3.3.243–83**

Read the given extract and then answer the question.

Explore the significance of this extract to the tragedy of *Othello*. Include in your answer analysis of Shakespeare's dramatic methods.

In conclusion, my opinion of Othello has changed during this scene because he has already changed from the beginning of the play since he referred to Desdemona as a 'fair warrior' showing that he loves her a lot at this point and she is always going to love him as she called him 'sweet'. This is ironic as Iago works away at Othello and changes his love for her so far that he loses all his tragic dignity and then kills her. Shakespeare engineers this change so that Othello believes he has been betrayed by everyone and he starts to act emotionally.

I can see this even in this scene because by the end of it he really trusts Iago when he should be trusting his wife. Iago's tactics are to sow seeds of doubt in Othello's mind and then let them fester. Othello speaks in a soliloquy here that sets the scene for what is going to happen later. His language has changed which is tragic and shows he has lost all sense of nobility.

Student F

This task also comes from an answer to the following possible task from AQA Specification B Paper 1:

Othello **3.3.243–83**

Read the given extract and then answer the question.

Explore the significance of this extract to the tragedy of *Othello*. Include in your answer analysis of Shakespeare's dramatic methods.

In this extract, Shakespeare has carefully balanced Iago's Machiavellian plotting against Othello's fatal descent into self-doubt. Iago's urgent instructions and Othello's anguished soliloquy are both focused on Desdemona, absent but central to their thoughts. Ironically, it is Desdemona who is next going to enter onto the stage and commit the crucial but accidental error of dropping her handkerchief. Struggles for power and the pains of romantic love have been shown to be crucial forces in the play.

Act 3, Scene 3 is a pivotal scene, and this extract a pivotal moment in that scene. By the end of the scene, Othello seems to have fallen irredeemably into Iago's hands. 'Now art thou my lieutenant' he says, ironically rewarding Iago with the office which – having been denied it – fuelled Iago's hate. 'I am your own for ever' replies Iago, chillingly, and the stage is set for Othello's inevitable tragic downfall.

Examiner's commentary

This student:

- ◥ Establishes a clear and meaningful connection between the extract and the wider context of the play **(A01)**.
- ◥ Brings the essay to an assured close with a wider sense of the movement of the whole play and sharp use of quotation.
- ◥ Makes confident judgements: 'shown to be crucial forces'.
- ◥ Comments very perceptively on aspects of dramatic structure within the extract and the scene as a whole, e.g. the careful balance between Iago's speeches and those of Othello **(A02)**.
- ◥ Offers sophisticated judgement about the relevance of certain contexts, e.g. power and love **(A03)**.
- ◥ Connects texts through clear reference to aspects of tragedy **(A04)**.
- ◥ Argues for the significance of the scene in terms of the tragedy of *Othello* **(A05)**.

If the rest of this essay reached this level of performance, this student should be on course to achieve a mark that equates to an A grade.

Building skills 2: Analysing texts in detail

Having worked through the previous section on structuring your writing, this section contains a range of annotated extracts from students' responses that will enable you to assess the extent to which these students have successfully demonstrated their writing skills and mastery of the assessment objectives. Each extract comes with a commentary to help you identify what each student is doing well and/or what changes they would need to make to their writing to target a higher grade.

The main focus here is on the ways in which you can successfully include analysis of language, structure and form to gain high marks for Assessment Objective 2.

Student A

This sample comes from an answer to the following possible examination task from AQA 'B' A-level English Literature specification, Paper 1.

Read the given extract and then answer the question.

Explore the significance of this extract (3.3.326–64) to the tragedy of *Othello*. Include in your answer analysis of Shakespeare's dramatic methods.

> IAGO I will in Cassio's lodging lose this napkin,
> And let him find it. Trifles light as air
> Are to the jealous confirmations strong
> As proofs of holy writ: this may do something.
> The Moor already changes with my poison:
> Dangerous conceits are, in their natures, poisons.
> Which at the first are scarce found to distaste,
> But with a little act upon the blood.
> Burn like the mines of Sulphur. I did say so:
> Look, where he comes!
>
> Re-enter OTHELLO
>
> Not poppy, nor mandragora,
> Nor all the drowsy syrups of the world,
> Shall ever medicine thee to that sweet sleep
> Which thou owedst yesterday.
>
> OTHELLO Ha! ha! false to me?
>
> IAGO Why, how now, general! no more of that.

OTHELLO Avaunt! be gone! thou hast set me on the rack:
I swear 'tis better to be much abused
Than but to know't a little.

IAGO How now, my lord!

OTHELLO What sense had I of her stol'n hours of lust?
I saw't not, thought it not, it harm'd not me:
I slept the next night well, was free and merry;
I found not Cassio's kisses on her lips:
He that is robb'd, not wanting what is stol'n,
Let him not know't, and he's not robb'd at all.

IAGO I am sorry to hear this.

OTHELLO I had been happy, if the general camp,
Pioneers and all, had tasted her sweet body,
So I had nothing known. O, now, for ever
Farewell the tranquil mind! farewell content!
Farewell the plumed troop, and the big wars,
That make ambition virtue! O, farewell!
Farewell the neighing steed, and the shrill trump,
The spirit-stirring drum, the ear-piercing fife,
The royal banner, and all quality,
Pride, pomp and circumstance of glorious war!
And, O you mortal engines, whose rude throats
The immortal Jove's dead clamours counterfeit,
Farewell! Othello's occupation's gone!

IAGO Is't possible, my lord?

Here the tragedy of *Othello* results not simply from weakness of character, or hamartia, but from an accident of fate. Iago, as often, is able to improvise and turn events to his advantage. In his opening soliloquy he characteristically informs the audience of his intentions, to change Othello 'with my poison'. His speeches are filled with the imagery of poison and suggestions of the tortures of hell, 'burn like the mines of sulphur'.

But Iago does more than this. Acting like a stage manager or analyst of a play of his own devising, he directly comments on Othello's entrance. In an ironic echo of some of the characteristic rhythms and verbal patterns of Othello's speech, he draws attention to how far he has transformed Othello from the noble

Moor of the opening scenes. Othello now talks Iago's language. He speaks of 'the rack', 'stolen hours of lust' and pioneers tasting 'her sweet body'. Torn by anguished despair, he gives way to a burst of rhetorical self-dramatisation, falling back on a sad echo of his heroic vocabulary: 'Farewell the tranquil mind, farewell content'.

This is a (perhaps self-indulgent) tragic farewell to his previous life. The culmination of the speech with the words 'Othello's reputation's gone' throws some light on one of his, and the play's, preoccupations – public respect. This is a concept which occupies the thoughts of Cassio and Iago, as well as Othello. His bitter fantasy about even the 'pioneers' enjoying Desdemona's body draws its power from the lowly status of such soldiers.

If a sense of personal honour and dignity is a driving force in the play, then so is knowledge – and self-knowledge. Othello bitterly claims that it would have been better if he 'had nothing known' and that it is 'better to be much abus'd/Than but to know't a little'. But the point is that his present 'knowledge' is based on a fiction. When he knew Desdemona to be a true and loving wife, then he had real knowledge. Now he has only a delusion.

Examiner's commentary:

A01   Confident and informed response. Perceptive use of associated concepts and terminology. Well integrated quotations used to support relevant points.

A02   Close detailed analysis of dramatic language and structure and the ways in which Shakespeare uses them to shape meaning.

A03   Awareness of the significance of the different context in which the text was written.

A04   Implicitly explores links with other tragedies.

A05   Offers different interpretations of the significance of Othello's speeches.

If the rest of the essay reached this level of performance it is likely the student would be on course to achieve a notional grade A.

Student B

This sample comes from an answer to the following possible examination task from AQA 'A' A-level English Literature specification, Paper 1.

Many texts show the destructive power of jealousy in love relationships.

In the light of this view, discuss how Shakespeare presents the operation of jealousy in this extract and elsewhere in the play.

DESDEMONA Something, sure, of state,
Either from Venice, or some unhatched practice
Made demonstrable here in Cyprus to him,
Hath puddled his clear spirit: and in such cases
Men's natures wrangle with inferior things,
Though great ones are their object. 'Tis even so;
For let our finger ache, and it indues
Our other healthful members even to that sense
Of pain: nay, we must think men are not gods,
Nor of them look for such observances
As fit the bridal. Beshrew me much, Emilia,
I was, unhandsome warrior as I am,
Arraigning his unkindness with my soul;
But now I find I had suborn'd the witness,
And he's indicted falsely.

EMILIA Pray heaven it be state-matters, as you think,
And no conception nor no jealous toy
Concerning you.

DESDEMONA Alas the day! I never gave him cause.

EMILIA But jealous souls will not be answered so;
They are not ever jealous for the cause,
But jealous for they are jealous: 'tis a monster
Begot upon itself, born on itself.

DESDEMONA Heaven keep that monster from Othello's mind!

EMILIA Lady, amen.

DESDEMONA I will go seek him. Cassio, walk hereabout:
If I do find him fit, I'll move your suit
And seek to effect it to my uttermost.

CASSIO I humbly thank your ladyship.

Exeunt DESDEMONA and EMILIA

Enter BIANCA

BIANCA Save you, friend Cassio!

CASSIO What make you from home?
How is it with you, my most fair Bianca?
I' faith, sweet love, I was coming to your house.

BIANCA And I was going to your lodging, Cassio.
What, keep a week away? seven days and nights?
Eight score eight hours? and lovers' absent hours,
More tedious than the dial eight score times?
O weary reckoning!

CASSIO Pardon me, Bianca:
I have this while with leaden thoughts been pressed:
But I shall, in a more continuate time,
Strike off this score of absence. Sweet Bianca,

Giving her DESDEMONA's handkerchief

Take me this work out.

BIANCA O Cassio, whence came this?
This is some token from a newer friend:
To the felt absence now I feel a cause:
Is't come to this? Well, well.

CASSIO Go to, woman!
Throw your vile guesses in the devil's teeth,
From whence you have them. You are jealous now
That this is from some mistress, some remembrance:
No, in good troth, Bianca.

BIANCA Why, whose is it?

CASSIO I know not, sweet: I found it in my chamber.
I like the work well: ere it be demanded –
As like enough it will – I'ld have it copied:
Take it, and do't; and leave me for this time.

(3.4.137–89)

Desdemona's speech to Emilia, just after Iago has left the stage,
introduces a scene that presents two very different forms of
jealousy. Her opening words offer a sad realisation that Othello
is merely human after all, 'Men are not gods', and she ironically
proceeds to seek some other cause than jealousy for his aberrant
behaviour. She focuses her attention on Othello the public man,
troubled by affairs of state, but the 'unhatched practice' she
mentions is closer to home. It is Emilia, oddly disinclined to
acknowledge her own responsibility for Othello's anger, who
returns to the question of jealousy with the dismissive remark
about a 'jealous toy'. 'Is not this man jealous?' she has previously
asked, and develops her own exploration of the idea by
concluding that jealousy has a self-perpetuating quality. Jealous
souls are 'jealous for they are jealous'. This conclusion could, of
course, be seen as self-exculpation; her own role in removing the
handkerchief is conveniently ignored.

Emilia's description of jealousy as 'a monster' ironically echoes
Iago's words in the previous scene, and without knowing it she
has become an accomplice in her husband's plans. It is also ironic
that Iago himself seems motivated by jealousy at many points
in the play. He claims to be jealous of Othello as a rival for his
wife's love; he obsessively broods over the office of lieutenant
that Cassio holds; some readings of the play suggest that he is
motivated by a homosexual desire for Othello and is thus also
jealous of Desdemona.

During her conversation with Emilia, Desdemona herself has
little to say; she seems crushed by her misfortune. Too late, and
with tragic irony, she prays that heaven will keep the 'monster'
of jealousy 'from Othello's mind'. Her innocence is demonstrated
in her final promise to Cassio that she will plead his cause.

When Desdemona and Emilia leave the stage we witness another
demonstration of jealousy, serious in its own way, but with
elements of comedy. Bianca's shrill protestations to Cassio form a
sharp contrast with Desdemona's restraint. She is, nevertheless,
also a victim of jealousy, and also focused on the handkerchief.
Iago's earlier words 'I will in Cassio's lodging lose this napkin'
are shown to have had speedy effect. Things are happening very
quickly at this stage in the play.

Examiner's commentary:

A01 Confident and informed response. Perceptive use of associated concepts and terminology. Well integrated quotations used to support relevant points.

A02 Close detailed analysis of language, structure and form and the ways in which Shakespeare uses them to shape meaning.

A03 Relevant and considered reference to moral contexts.

A04 Explores a relevant link with the issue of love through the ages in connection with the central focus of the task and ranges effectively around the play.

A05 Suggests different interpretations of Emilia's behaviour and other attitudes to jealousy.

If the rest of the essay reached this level of performance it is likely the student would be on course to achieve a notional grade A.

Student C

This sample comes from an answer to the following possible task from the Edexcel A-level English Literature specification, Component 1.

Explore Shakespeare's presentation of innocence in *Othello*.

You must relate your discussion to relevant contextual factors and ideas from your critical reading.

Shakespeare's presentation of innocence in the 'bed scene' of *Othello* seems to support David Scott Kastan's comment that tragedy deals with 'uncompensated suffering'. Ironically, it is Othello who uses the language of Christianity, with references to prayer, heaven, and soul, rather than the innocent Desdemona. He seems to see himself as a minister of divine justice, and this shows itself in the formality of his speech. This is, though, a role that he has created for himself. An audience is unlikely to see things in the same way.

The dialogue with Desdemona as she lies on what is to be her deathbed is swiftly alternating, revealing the huge gap in understanding between the wife and her husband. Desdemona is treated like a criminal suspect — which she is in Othello's eyes. Her direct questioning of Othello has, with tragic irony, come too late. Also ironic is the sense that it is partly her innocence which destroys her, as Iago has prophesied earlier in the play, 'So will I turn her virtue into pitch'. Her generous concern for Cassio's fate is taken by Othello as a sign of her guilt.

Her terrified description of Othello's appearance, 'why gnaw you so your nether lip?' is partly for the audience's benefit, but also reveals her innocent vulnerability. She is trapped alone; the witnesses to the crime that Othello is about to commit are at present just off-stage.

Examiner's commentary:

A01 Uses appropriate terminology and quotations, bearing in mind that this is an open book examination paper. The argument is coherent.

A02 Some attempt made to analyse language and the ways in which Shakespeare uses words to shape meaning. Some ideas could be further developed. Understanding of stagecraft is evident.

A03 Clear understanding of the relevance of contexts of Christianity and dramatic tragedy.

A04 No connection with another text required in this answer.

A05 Different interpretations suggested with reference to the critical anthology. These could have been explored further.

If the rest of the essay reached this level of performance the student would be on course to achieve a notional grade B.

Extended commentaries

Commentary 1

Act 1, Scene 1: The opening of the play

TASK

How is Iago presented in the first 65 lines of the play? What readings of the character are made possible in this opening scene?

It is characteristic of many Shakespearean tragedies that the main protagonist does not appear in the opening scene. This would seem to be the case here, although there has been some debate about whether Iago could be seen as the true hero of *Othello*.

Certainly Iago dominates this scene from the beginning. Some productions have Iago rather apologetically following Roderigo onto the stage, but if this suggests subordination then that impression doesn't last long. Roderigo is quickly reduced to brief comments and interjections – 'I would not follow him then' – that hardly hold up Iago's unstoppable flow of words.

Iago's favourite subject seems to be Iago. The number of times he uses the words 'I' or 'me' in the opening speeches reveals his self-absorption. But one of the important ways he sees himself is as being different from other people. He is not 'almost damned in a fair wife' like Cassio; he is not 'a duteous and knee-crooking knave' like other servants; and crucially he is not like Othello: 'were I the Moor, I would not be Iago'.

So what does Iago seem to be? This is a difficult question to answer, and this difficulty itself says something important about Iago – his slippery, evasive nature: 'I am not what I am'. Coleridge famously talked of Iago's 'motiveless malignity', but there is surely an argument that he has, if anything, too many motives, and several of these emerge in this scene.

Iago seems to be consumed by envy and jealousy, which is ironic bearing in mind that it is the emotion of jealousy that he uses to destroy Othello. He sees himself as an old soldier, unjustly overlooked for promotion, 'Preferment goes by letter and affection/And not by old gradation'. Promotion is given instead to a 'great arithmetician', an amateur who fights by the book, and who is – to make things worse – an outsider, a Florentine. Iago's later manipulation of events to deprive Cassio of his position is part of his plan to revenge himself on Othello, but in doing so he also revenges himself on Cassio and steps into his place – which he feels he should have had from the beginning: 'I know my price, I am worth no worse a place'. Iago is always conscious of being Iago.

He is presented as being very conscious of place and position, and makes many references to the different degrees of rank and status, bitterly referring to himself as 'his Moorship's ancient'. He observes the relationships between masters and servants from a bitter, cynical angle:

We cannot all be masters, nor all masters

Cannot be truly followed

(1.1.43–44)

He will not be such a servant, 'Whip me such honest knaves'. Iago's use of the word 'knaves' is ironic here. Knave can mean 'menial', but also 'villain'. Dishonest knaves would ordinarily be more likely to be punished by whipping. As often, Iago turns conventional morality on its head. He clearly has his own agenda, which often seems to suggest a considerable interest in money. We immediately learn that he has been taking money from Roderigo; his scornful comments about Cassio are phrased in the language of accountancy: 'debitor and creditor'; he admires those servants who have 'lined their coats'. *Othello* is often seen as a play that is driven by the motive of sexual jealousy. Iago also seems to be motivated by an obsession with rank and fortune.

It might seem that this list of unpleasant qualities means that Iago can only attract a very hostile response from the beginning. However, this fails to take into account the fact that at this stage the audience has not seen Othello and cannot be sure that Iago's contempt is not justified, that Othello, for instance, has not been unjust in his failure to acknowledge Iago's qualities and service, and is indeed too full of self-love and 'bombast'. It is also possible to be rather attracted by Iago's energetic and colourful language, his penetrating observations about people and life in general. From the beginning of the play he is presented as a shaper of narratives, with a very strong – if at times bitter – sense of the gap between appearance and reality. This doubt that 'the outward action does demonstrate the native act' lies at the heart of drama itself.

Iago is in many ways a very powerful stage presence and attracts our interest and attention from the start, certainly in comparison to the limp and unimpressive Roderigo. As an audience, we may at this point suspend judgement. What Iago has certainly done is to make us eager to see what happens next.

Commentary 2
Act 3, Scene 3

> ### TASK
> 'In the tragedy of *Othello*, jealousy and deception work together as destructive forces.'
> Bearing in mind this view, discuss the significance of jealousy and deception in this extract and elsewhere in the play.

Deceit and jealousy lie at the heart of the tragic experience of *Othello*, but the way they operate is complex and many-sided. Jealousy, for instance, is an emotion experienced by several characters in different ways, while deliberate deception of others operates alongside self-deception.

In this extract, the scene is structured around Iago's careful dropping of the seeds of jealousy into Othello's mind and then nurturing their growth. Just before this extract, Iago has hypocritically warned Othello to 'beware' jealousy as a 'green-eyed monster'. The concept of jealousy dominates the opening stages of this extract. Othello's first speech has the word 'jealousy' placed at the beginning, in the middle and at the end, framing and binding the speech around this central idea.

Iago's use of the idea of jealousy is driven by his devious and manipulative tactics. His opening manoeuvres involve the use of what appear as proverbial sayings, such as 'poor and content is rich and rich enough', to create an impression of common sense wisdom. He concludes his first speech with a rhetorical appeal, delivered in the sort of language likely to appeal to Othello, rich in religious and heroic imagery: 'Good heaven, the souls of all my tribe defend/from jealousy!'

Othello's response is to deny that he is given to jealousy. The irony of this assertion is reinforced by his claim in the final scene of the play that he is 'one not easily jealous'. There has been much critical debate around this statement. Certainly, there is no doubt that Othello succumbs to jealousy of the most extreme kind, but it could be argued (indeed A.C. Bradley has done so) that the reason for this is more to do with Iago's remarkable powers as a tempter figure than with Othello's own innate weakness. Even at the end of the play, Othello continues to insist that he was 'one not easily jealous'. Within this scene, significantly, a certain structural change takes place. Othello's rather theatrical denial that he is naturally jealous occupies a speech of fifteen lines, full of rhetorical effects that might allow him temporarily to dominate the stage. After this speech, however, Iago's growing power can be seen in his own increasing control of the exchanges. His are the longer speeches; Othello is increasingly reduced to terse, even monosyllabic responses – 'Not a jot, not a jot'. He has now become an audience to Iago's extended representations of 'reality'; he will soon become an actor in a play of Iago's own devising

The contextual issues that lie behind Othello's possible jealousy are also important factors here. In the opening scenes of the play, Othello is presented as a commanding, self-possessed figure, but his position is perhaps less stable than it first appears, and Iago is able to play on this instability. All Othello's previous experience, by his own account, has been in public affairs and on the battlefield, where what Iago here calculatingly calls 'his free and noble nature' could operate outside any of the complex constraints of civilian or domestic life. Othello himself has earlier acknowledged that had it not been for his passion for Desdemona 'the sea's worth' would not have tempted him to restrict his 'unhoused free condition'. He is presented as being simply unfamiliar with marriage relationships, and Iago plays on this, hinting at the 'pranks' that Venetian women characteristically employ to deceive their husbands.

In addition, Othello is an outsider, a free and wheeling stranger' as Roderigo scornfully calls him whose life has been spent abroad in 'feats of broil and battle'. Iago suggests that he does not understand 'our country disposition'. He is operating in unfamiliar territory. Towards the end of this extract Iago even risks the suggestion that Othello's relationship with Desdemona – and her part in it – is 'unnatural' and 'rank' – his very racial background is used to encourage him to jealousy. Othello is also an old man who has married a young wife, often a subject for comic ridicule in Elizabethan (and other) drama. Later in this scene he bitterly acknowledges that '**I am declined into the vale of years**'. With savage irony, Iago also turns Desdemona's brave defiance of her father – in support of her loyalty to Othello – against her, arguing that it was not a sign of her love but of her capacity for deceit: 'She did deceive her father marrying you'. He turns one of Othello's greatest triumphs against him.

It should be pointed out that Othello is not the only character given to jealousy. Iago can clearly be seen as being jealous of not only Cassio, but Desdemona and Othello himself. Some actors (such as Ian McKellen and Simon Russell Beale) have portrayed Iago as being partially motivated by repressed homosexual desires, and there is no doubt that his view of sexual relations seems constantly twisted and anguished. On a more comic level, Bianca seems always to be torn by her jealousy of Cassio's other lovers. If Othello's was the only jealousy in the play, and if it had no good background reason, then it would be much harder for any audience to see him as having any of the worth and nobility that we associate with tragic heroes.

Top ten quotation

What tragic heroes also often show, however, is a lack of self-awareness and there is plenty of evidence of this failing in this extract and elsewhere in the play. Othello's jealousy is activated by Iago's deception, but there is an argument that Othello also deceives himself, perhaps even to the extent that he considers himself suited to marriage at all. There is a bitter sense in the play that love can be seen as a weakness as well as a strength, and can be used to deceive; Iago speaks in this scene of his 'love' for Othello at the same time as he deliberately manipulates him. However, within this extract Othello also contradicts his own view of himself.' I'll see before I doubt', he says, and 'when I doubt, prove'. But this is exactly what he does not do. By the end of this extract he prepares to rely on what Iago can 'perceive' and even encourages him to 'set on thy wife to observe'. He places a dreadful confidence in what 'this honest creature doubtless sees and knows', not on his own capacity for judgement.

'Seeing' is an important concept in *Othello*, trusting in appearances rather than what is truly the case. Othello is not the only character shown as being the prey of jealousy and deceit, but the combination of these two forces makes him the victim as well as the hero of the tragedy.

IAGO: … I am not what I am. (I.1.64)

1

> From the start Iago reveals to the audience that he is duplicitous, thus making it complicit and drawing attention to how gullible all the other characters are for not being able to see through him. The themes of false appearances and faulty judgement are thus introduced in the first scene, and Iago is presented as a dangerous vice figure.

IAGO: How am I then a villain
To counsel Cassio to this parallel course,
Directly to his good? Divinity of hell!
When devils will the blackest sins put on,
They do suggest at first with heavenly shows,
As I do now… (2.3.333–8)

2

> From the beginning of the play, Iago has suggested that he is not to be taken at face value ('I am not what I am'). Here, in a soliloquy, he rather teases the audience with an acknowledgement of his complex duplicity. A challenging rhetorical question leads into a sort of internal dialogue in which he gleefully provides his own answer. His speech is characteristically full of diabolic imagery: 'hell', 'devils' and 'sins'. The juxtaposition of 'blackest sins' against 'heavenly shows' continues the black/white opposition that runs through the play. It also develops the important theme of appearance and reality. Iago defiantly establishes himself as the tragic villain of the play, and Cassio is presented as yet another of his dupes.

OTHELLO: Excellent wretch! Perdition catch my soul,
But I do love thee! and when I love thee not,
Chaos is come again. (3.3. 91–3)

3

> 'Wretch' need not be taken negatively here; it was often a term of endearment. The timing of this speech by Othello is significant. It occurs at the start of the long scene during which his feelings for Desdemona are fatally corrupted by Iago. His expression of undying love at this point is thus bitterly ironic. The word 'but' allows for different readings of this line: Othello would risk damnation for his love, or deserve damnation if he ceases to love. Either way, the tragic significance of his utter dependence on his love for Desdemona is made clear. Love has by now been established as a central force in the play.

4

OTHELLO: Haply, for I am black
And have not those soft parts of conversation
That chamberers have, or for I am declined
Into the vale of years,– yet that's not much –
She's gone. I am abused; and my relief
Must be to loathe her. (3.3.266–71)

This extract is taken from one of Othello's soliloquies. Some readings of the play have argued that his soliloquies lack the dramatic power of Iago's, and this makes it more difficult to see Othello as the tragic hero of the play. Here he is starting to see himself as his enemies do. Tragic heroes often experience a form of *anagnorisis*, a realisation of the mistakes they have made or the true nature of things. This is a false revelation; Othello's recognition of the truth is still to come.

5

EMILIA to DESDEMONA about men: They are all but stomachs, and we all but food … (III.4.105).

Emilia is giving a low, bestial view of relationships and sex, one she has presumably acquired by being Iago's wife. It is Iago's world view that is gradually imposed on the play, and on many of the characters. This quotation also makes explicit that women are passive and the victims of men, eaten and therefore destroyed by them. This idea foreshadows Emilia's fate as well as Desdemona's.

6

OTHELLO to DESDEMONA: Was this fair paper, this most goodly book,
Made to write 'whore' upon? What committed!
Committed! (4.2.71–3)

Othello bitterly picks up Desdemona's innocent but unfortunate query as to what sin she has 'committed'. He takes 'committed' only in terms of its connection with 'adultery'. From being the woman on whom his whole life and sense of self-worth was centred, Desdemona has now in his eyes degenerated into 'whore'. Once thought of as 'fair' and unsullied, she is now seen as a 'book', a passive object that can be categorised by a male reader. Ironically, Othello proves himself incapable of interpreting the 'text' that is Desdemona. Iago has substituted his own reading.

DESDEMONA to EMILIA: My mother had a maid called Barbary;
She was in love, and he she loved proved mad,
And did forsake her. She had a 'Song of Willow'—
An old thing 'twas, but it expressed her fortune,
And she died singing it. That song tonight
Will not go from my mind. (4.3.19–24)

7

> This scene marks a temporary lessening in the tension before the great climactic action of the last act. The reference to 'Barbary' ironically recalls Iago's description of Othello as a 'Barbary horse' in Act 1. Emilia echoes Desdemona's words on her deathbed, and the willow, here and elsewhere in Shakespeare's plays, is associated with the suffering of unrequited love. There is a strongly elegiac tone to this speech and the scene as a whole. This scene is sometimes used as evidence for a reading of Desdemona as a simple, innocent victim; other readings see her as a far more spirited character.

OTHELLO: It is the cause, it is the cause, my soul,—
Let me not name it to you, you chaste stars!:
It is the cause. (5.2.1–3)

8

> There has been much debate as to whether Othello regains tragic grandeur in the final scene. The 'cause' is ambiguous; it may be that we are encouraged to see Othello's sense of his own motivation as uncertain, or that 'the cause' has somehow assumed a huge power that is impossible to name or withstand. He seems to be suggesting that Desdemona's sin is so vile that even to name it would offend the 'chaste' stars above. Ironically, though, Emilia's final defence of Desdemona insists that she was 'chaste', and Othello in his final grasp of the truth speaks of her 'chastity.' A focus on sexual loyalty and betrayal is a characteristic of many domestic tragedies.

IAGO: Demand me nothing; what you know, you know:
From this time forth I never will speak word. (5.2.300–1)

9

> Iago is unusual among Shakespearean heroes and villains in that he does not die before the end of the play. Much of his power has been in his command of language, and words have often seemed to spill out of him during the play. His final enigmatic refusal to speak is thus all the more striking. It also emphasises the degree to which he and his motives have never been easy to pin down, and are finally unknowable. As often in tragedies, we are left with a sense of the mystery and uncertainty of human life.

10

OTHELLO about himself: ... one that loved not wisely, but too well ... (V.2.342)

▼ This self-aggrandising judgement of Othello suggests that he has returned to the heroic view of himself he held at the beginning, and which won Desdemona's heart. It is a dubious assertion that he loved 'too well', as he ultimately placed his trust in Iago's words rather than those of Desdemona. It could be argued that in this speech Othello is attempting to write his own obituary, and excuse his terrible actions as 'unlucky deeds'. An alternative reading would argue that he here regains some heroic stature.

TASK
Go back through the text and select your own 'top ten' quotations. Comment on each one to justify its inclusion, showing how it is important within the play.

Books

A vast number of books have been written about the plays of Shakespeare, both individual plays and general studies. The best collections of studies of *Othello* are:

Barton, A. 'His tragedies' in Christopher Hicks (ed.), *The Penguin History of English Literature: English Drama to 1700*, Harmondsworth: Penguin, 1993, pp. 197–233 – Barton's essay her offers a helpful overview of *Othello* in the canon of Shakespearean tragedy.

Cowen, L.C. (ed.) (2004) *Othello: New Casebooks*, London: Palgrave Macmillan – A very useful anthology, including examples of post-colonial and feminist criticism

Dollimore, J. and Sinfield, A. (eds.) (1985) *Political Shakespeare: New essays in Cultural Materialism*, Manchester: Manchester University Press – A helpful guide to understanding a Cultural Materialist approach to Shakespeare.

Heath, M. (ed. and tr.) (1996) *Aristotle: Poetics*, Harmondsworth: Penguin – This contains all of Aristotle's theory on tragedy.

Honigmann, E. A. J. (1996) *Othello*, Arden Shakespeare – The introduction to this new Arden edition is an outstanding critical study of the play, its context, sources and stage history.

Howard, J.E. and O'Conner, M.F. (eds.) (1987) *Shakespeare Reproduced: The Text in History*, London: Routledge – Howard and O' Connor's volume contains several essays on Shakespeare including Karen Newman's classic work on *Othello*.

McEvoy, S. *Shakespeare: The Basics*. London: Routledge, 2000 – This is a very useful introduction to the works of Shakespeare.

Ridler, A. (ed.) (1970) *Shakespearean Criticism 1935–1970*, Oxford: Oxford University Press – Ridler offers a collection of useful criticism from this period.

Wain, J. (ed.) (1971) *Othello: A Casebook*, Macmillan – An excellent anthology of criticism of the play, giving a historical overview of the changing attitudes to the play from contemporary to present-day through extracts from critics from different centuries.

Recommended general studies are:

- Bayley, J. (1981) *Shakespeare and Tragedy*, Routledge – A very useful critical study of the tragedies.
- Honigmann, E. A. J. (1976) *Shakespeare: Seven Tragedies*, Macmillan – Honigmann is a leading critic who edited the new Arden edition.

❧ Kermode, F. (2000) *Shakespeare's Language*, Allen Lane – An up-to-date and readable study of Shakespeare's language use.

❧ Leech, C. (1969) *Tragedy, the Critical Idiom* series, general editor John D. Jump, Routledge – A useful study of the genre of tragedy.

❧ Lerner, L. (ed.) (1963) *Shakespeare's Tragedies*, Penguin – A classic study of all Shakespeare's tragedies.

❧ Muir, K. (1972) *Shakespeare's Tragic Sequence*, Hutchinson University Library – A perceptive and stimulating essay on the tragedies.

❧ Neely, C. T. (1985) *Broken Nuptials in Shakespeare's Plays*, University of Illinois Press – A striking feminist interpretation of the plays.

More recent and radical views of the play may be found, for example:

❧ 'A Post-Colonial Critique of Othello' by Gregory Schneider at: www.associatedcontent.com/article/14697/a_postcolonial_critique_of_othello.html?cat=9

❧ 'The Black Other in Elizabethan Drama' by Stacy Coyne at: www.associatedcontent.com/article/31627/shakespeares_othello_the_black_other.html?cat=38

❧ 'Interpreting Racial Imagery in O' by Os Davis at: www.associatedcontent.com/article/28023/interpreting_racial_imagery_in_o.html?cat=38

Podcasts

University of Oxford Podcasts: podcasts.ox.ac.uk/othello

– Emma Smith's *Approaching Shakespeare* Series, looking in particular at the question of race.

University of Warwick podcasts: www2.warwick.ac.uk/newsandevents/podcasts/culture/22-othello-audio

– Professor Carol Rutter and Patrice Naiambana on *Othello* and the diasporic experience.

Films

Othello has proved a popular subject for film-makers from the birth of the industry. No fewer than four silent black-and-white versions were made between 1907 and 1922, and at least another 15 films have been made since then. Particularly memorable productions include:

1952: directed by Orson Welles, who also took the part of Othello, with Micheal MacLiammoir as Iago. Available on DVD.

1964: directed by Stuart Burge, John Dexter's stage production with Laurence Olivier (blacked up) as Othello and Frank Finlay as Iago. Available on DVD.

1981: BBC Shakespeare, directed by Jonathan Miller, with Anthony Hopkins (blacked up) as Othello and Bob Hoskins as Iago, with a cockney accent. Available on DVD.

1986: Film version of Verdi's opera of *Otello*, directed by Franco Zeffirelli, with Placido Domingo as Otello and Justino Diaz as Iago. Available on DVD.

1987: South African version directed by Janet Suzman during apartheid. John Kani plays Othello and Richard Haddon Haines plays Iago.

1989: American version directed by Ted Lange, who also played Othello, with Hawthorne James as Iago.

1993: Royal Shakespeare Company's 1989 production directed by Trevor Nunn, with Willard White as Othello and Iago played by Ian McKellen as a working-class outsider. Available on DVD.

1995: Oliver Parker's film with Kenneth Branagh as Iago and Laurence Fishburne, the first big-screen black Othello. Available on DVD.

2001: A modern version of *Othello*, set in an American school, with updated dialogue but otherwise close to the original. Directed by Tim Blake Nelson with Mekhi Phifer as Othello (renamed Odin) and Josh Hartnett as Iago (also renamed). Available on DVD.

2001: A modern television version, directed by Geoffrey Sax and set in the Metropolitan police force, starring Eamonn Walker as John Othello and Christopher Eccleston as Ben Jago. Available on DVD.

2007: A filmed version of the production at the Globe Theatre, starring Eamonn Walker as Othello (again; see above) and Tim McInnerny as Iago. Directed by Wilson Milam and Derek Bailey. Available on DVD.

2013: This is a screening of a stage production, directed by Nicholas Hytner for National Theatre Live, with Adrian Lester as Othello and Rory Kinnear as Iago.

Weblinks

There are a vast number of sites on the internet with material on Shakespeare and *Othello*. Here are some of the most useful:

- **http://shakespeare.palomar.edu/** *Mr William Shakespeare and the Internet* is one of the best general Shakespeare sites. It includes general information and an extensive set of links to other sites, many of which include the full text of some or all of the plays, listed at **http://shakespeare. palomar.edu/works.htm**

- **www.eamesharlan.org/tptt/** This site includes a word count, and line count by character, for each play.

- **http://absoluteshakespeare.com/guides/othello/othello.htm** includes Coleridge's famous essay on the play.

- **www.unibas.ch/shine/linkstragothellowf.html** lists resources.
- **http://web.uvic.ca/shakespeare/Annex/DraftTxt/Oth/index.htm** has texts of the Quarto and Folio accessible by scene or by page.
- **www.shakespeare-online.com/essays/othelloessays.html** contains a good collection of essays on *Othello*.
- **www.clicknotes.com/othello/Osource.html** includes the text of Cinthio's tale upon which Othello is based.
- **www.shakespeares-globe.org/** is the official website of the reconstructed Globe Theatre.
- **www.shakespeare.org.uk** is the site of the Shakespeare Birthplace Trust.
- The Google Scholar site at **http://scholar.google.co.uk** has links to more than 44,000 articles which are allegedly about the play (search for 'Othello + Shakespeare' to exclude the game). Some have the complete text, others only part, but it is worth exploring.

Pictures of historical Othellos may be found at:

- www.colby.edu/personal/l/leosborn/othello.html